HIKING IN
BEAR
COUNTRY

HIKING IN BEAR COUNTRY

Keith Scott

NIMBUS
PUBLISHING LTD

Copyright © 1995, Keith Scott

All rights reserved. No part of this book covered by the copyrights hereon may be reproduced or used in any form or by any means—graphic, electronic, or mechanical—without the prior written permission of the publisher. Any request for photocopying, recording, taping, or information storage and retrieval systems of any part of this book shall be directed in writing to the Canadian Reprography Collective, 379 Adelaide Street West, Suite M1, Toronto, Ontario, M5V 1S5.

Nimbus Publishing Limited
P. O. Box 9301, Station A
Halifax, N. S.
B3K 5N5
(902)455-4286

Design: Doug Porter, Virtual Image Productions
Printed and bound in Canada

Canadian Cataloguing in Publication Data
Scott, Keith Vincent, 1936-
　　　Hiking in bear country
　　　　ISBN 1-55109-110-0
1. Bears.　2. Hiking -- Safety measures.　I. Title.
QL737.C27S36 1995　599.74,446　C95-950054-5

CONTENTS

Acknowledgments *vi*
Foreword *vii*
Introduction *ix*
1   The Bears I Know Best   *1*
2   Hiking In New Brunswick   *23*
3   Banff National Park   *29*
4   Jasper National Park   *43*
5   The Spatsizi Plateau   *61*
6   Spirit of the Rainforest   *69*
7   Hanna and Tintina Creeks, British Columbia   *75*
8   Kluane National Park, Yukon Territory   *79*
9   Chilcook Lake and Kodiak Island, Alaska   *87*
10   Fish Creek, Alaska   *97*
11   Denali National Park, Alaska   *117*
12   Polar Bear Country   *129*
13   The Bear Man's Safety Rules   *137*

Acknowledgments

I owe my deepest thanks to my mother, Dorothy Scott, who introduced me to the pleasures of nature when I was a child growing up in New Brunswick. Without her influence, I never would have become interested in the outdoors. My interest in the woods was further reinforced by fishing trips with my father and my brother.

My family is wonderful, and I am particularly grateful to my wife, Frances, and my sons Donny and Steven, for putting up with many years of my peculiar interests and my odd behaviour while searching for bears. I would also like to thank Donny and his friend Linda Roulston for their help with the preparation of this book. My sister Shirley Scott-Hickman contributed drawings of events and encounters that I was unable to photograph; I appreciate her artistic expertise.

When I was a young man and working as a fish guardian at Big Salmon River, I learned what it meant to be a conservationist from William Wetmore. His dedication to nature is something I have always tried to emulate.

Of all my friends, Jim Kahl is very special. His enthusiasm and energy spark my interest each summer, as we prepare for another adventure. No one can make hiking in bad conditions more enjoyable than he can.

Foreword

Having Keith Scott as a father has been quite an experience. I grew up believing that all families spent most of their time hiking, fishing, and taking pictures of bears. Indeed, one of my earliest memories is of my mother Frances, my father, and I wading across a freezing-cold river deep in the heart of the Yukon. Crossing a river with water up to your waist was what I always thought having fun meant—and I was right. Our family has always enjoyed—and endured—the wilderness. My brother Steven, who has continued the family tradition, started early: when he was only nine, he hiked forty kilometres into the heart of bear country.

Frances and Steven Scott.

    People must assess their lives at some point, and choose a path that will make them happy; if the path is well chosen, they will better understand their part in the cycle of life. There are many who sit behind a desk most of their lives, dreaming of adventure. My father was once one of these people; however, his love for nature compelled him to abandon a safe life. Since then, he has lived a life most men only dream about—or dread. Being curious about bears is far from being a mainstream hobby, but fulfiling this interest is what has always made my father happy. Dad has landed in many precarious situations, but he thrives on the excitement. His life has been well chosen.

    I have accompanied my father on many trips, and on each one I have discovered something new and wonderful about the relationship between humanity and nature. Once, when hiking in the Rocky Mountains with my father, I recall coming to a lake where careless campers had tossed their garbage into the water. We spent the next few hours wading into the lake and removing the mess. This was the first time I realized what it meant to be concerned about nature.

Another time, at home, I saw a spider crawling across the carpet. The natural reaction might be to squish the crawling nuisance, but my father spent twenty minutes trying to get the spider onto a piece of newspaper, then he carefully took it outside. But that wasn't all—Dad spent the next ten minutes watching the spider to make sure it was O.K. This level of concern is a paradigm of my father's relationship with nature, which is in vast contrast to that of most people I have met. Nature is often considered an impediment to progress and is largely taken for granted. Few people think twice about getting rid of a bothersome tree—they think cutting it down will improve the view. The person who throws a chip bag out the window of his gas-guzzler is the same one who buys environmentally friendly detergent the next day.

My father was fighting for the protection of wildlife and their habitat long before it became politically correct—not by spewing environmental rhetoric, but by doing something. Jim Kahl, one of my father's good friends, expressed a belief shared by many people who know my father. "Over the years I have come to really trust Keith's knowledge of wildlife and his truly deep sense of commitment towards protecting them. He will commit to action, while others are content to talk."

Don Scott on one of his many adventures.

Each summer our adventures begin again, and I continue to learn new ways of appreciating nature. Although my father leads a curious life, it is both honest and admirable.

—Don Scott

Introduction

It was yet another beautiful day, the sort that one takes for granted during a month of hiking through the mountains. Although I had another ten kilometres to cover, I was already picturing a nice campfire and a calm night under the stars. Just then the daydream vanished, and the nightmare began—a mother bear was standing directly in my path, staring at me, her cub nearby.

Stumbling across a bear is never wise, especially a mother bear with a cub. Could this be the end of my adventures? I tried to tell myself everything was going to be all right, but I was in the unfortunate position of being able to confirm that every tooth of this charging grizzly

Charging sow grizzly.

was glistening. The yellow glow and the sunken face were not handsome, but I was hardly the one to criticize. Retreat was impossible; the furry terror was only a few metres away, and closing in fast.

As the bear paused to gather her strength for the coming blows, I offered a quick prayer to Saint Peter, clenched my fist, and closed my eyes. A moment passed. Was I already dead? I peeked. The grizzly and her cub had vanished; only a few swaying bushes showed that they had ever been there. I shook my head, thanked Saint Peter, and asked myself what I could possibly have been thinking when I passed up that desk job back east, opting for a "career" in the forest. Indeed, having been brought up in New Brunswick, it seems odd that I would ever develop a fascination for bears. Most of my youth was spent playing basketball, but between games I began to go hiking and fishing.

Years before, my mother had introduced my sister Shirley, my brother

Donald, and me to nature by taking us to the beaches near our home in Saint John, New Brunswick. The most memorable of those trips was the annual sojourn in Lakeville, where we would visit relatives and spend happy hours fishing and hiking. Back home, my passion for the outdoors became more intense as I took my bike and sought out new spots to catch speckled trout. At times, I got so excited that I would run from one fishing pool to the next in search of a trout.

My friends shared my passion for the outdoors, and we would often find ourselves on the side of some brook or pond. These fishing trips heightened my enthusiasm for the outdoors, opening my eyes to the many wonders that nature had to offer. Life was everywhere—turtles, frogs, and all kinds of insects, especially butterflies. Anything that moved fascinated me.

My early backwoods adventures took place in the southern part of New Brunswick, which might seem an unlikely place to have an experience that justifies the word *adventure,* but just the same, any trip into the woods puts you in the middle of the unknown. Despite my eagerness to explore the outdoors, I was often frightened of what might be lurking in the shadows. During these times even a glimpse of my own shadow was enough to make my heart pound. You can never be sure what might be waiting around the next bend in the trail, especially when you are young, and expect to encounter danger, but my greatest terror was that I might encounter that most-feared of all forest creatures—a grizzly. I soon discovered there are no grizzlies in Atlantic Canada, but there is a healthy population of black bears, which quickly replaced grizzlies on my list of animals to fear.

I had heard many bear stories, each with a common theme: an unfortunate person would see the bear, and then he would be eaten. Often the details were bloody, and my imagination would make these tales even worse than they were. It got so that bears came to represent all that was evil in the universe. Although my view has changed over the years, those early forays into the woods always awakened fearful thoughts. I was convinced that if I saw a bear, I would be immediately devoured, and I would stay awake all night while I was camping, nervously scanning the horizon for any signs of trouble.

I have learned over the years that most bear tales are either greatly exaggerated or completely false; usually, there is no reason to fear. Although I must admit that some of the more gory stories linger in the back of my mind, they have never stopped me from hiking in the woods—where the true nature of bears' behaviour has reinforced my respect for these remarkable animals.

My childhood excursions provided many fond memories, but my real wilderness education began when I left Atlantic Canada and visited the Rocky Mountains—the Promised Land for anyone who truly loves nature. By then, I considered myself a self-taught expert on the outdoors, but I soon discovered that I had a lot to learn; for example, that people in the western provinces are particularly fearful of bears. I was bombarded with horror stories from park rangers and wardens, usually conveying the message that bears in the area are known to attack and kill without provocation, and following up with details about some recent mauling that had occurred. The conclusion was that anyone who so much as glimpses a bear is in grave danger.

A monarch butterfly feeding on the nectar of a Devil's Paintbrush.

I began to wonder if there was any foundation for the negative portrayal of bears, and my growing scepticism sowed the seeds for a lifelong investigation during which I would find out firsthand whether bears really deserved their bad reputation. After all, it is people and not animals who act out of cruelty. I have read many detailed accounts of the barbaric treatment of bears and other animals by "civilized" human beings over the centuries. The Romans trained bears as gladiators and, in what must have been a sickening display, slaughtered them for the amusement of the spectators. Other ancient civilizations conducted ceremonies in which bears were captured alive, tortured with arrows and finally strangled. During the Middle Ages, a popular form of entertainment was to capture a grizzly bear alive, blind it, beat it until it was in a weakened state, then continue the "fun" by releasing dogs to maul the bear to death. More recently, outdoor arenas in California were used for a new "sport"—battles to the death between grizzlies and bulls. But of all the stories I have read, the one that most displays the cowardice of some men is a "sporting event" in which a team of horsemen lasso a grizzly bear, then rip the animal apart.

Considering this legacy, it should come as no surprise that we have inherited what almost seems to be a need for violence. Such stories even make one wonder if the bear is sometimes justified in taking human life; at the very least, they demonstrate where the evil truly lies. Although these sorts of activities no longer flourish, humans continue to inflict a great deal of abuse on animals. Every year, hunters brag to me about shooting a bear, while others, who have not made their first kill, smirk as they express their desire to get just one bear before they die. I fail to understand how anyone can derive satisfaction from needlessly killing an animal. What sadistic motives drive men to kill for pleasure? Clearly, our civilization must learn to suppress and eliminate these cruel desires.

Perhaps we could start by examining our attitude toward the concept of hunting. Nothing has influenced the decline of the bear population as much as the invention and distribution of guns, and the resulting popularity of bear hunting as a "sport." I believe it is at best questionable whether hunting is truly a sport. In any true sport, all parties involved stand an equal chance of winning the event, but there is no situation in which animals are on equal terms with hunters armed with firearms. Fighting a bear with a rifle is like fighting a tank with an atom bomb; the outcome is obvious, and neither courage nor bravery is displayed. Furthermore, the introduction of guns has led to the needless slaughter of thousands of bears—in the name of sport.

At one time, natives hunted for food and clothing; animals were respected and only killed to provide the necessities of life. After an animal was killed, it was thanked in a ceremony. In native cultures the death of an animal was seen as a necessary sacrifice. I believe that if hunting must occur there must be adequate justification. "Fun" or "sport" do not qualify. The hunters of today could learn a lot from native ways of life.

In August 1990, while hiking on Admiralty Island, Alaska, I saw two men and a woman hunting along a riverbank. I asked them what they were after, and one of the men replied: "Anything that moves." The ignorance of his response, I believe, is typical of those who kill for fun. I hope never to encounter any other hunters like those; I am tired of meeting cowards with guns.

Today, as in the past, the livestock and lumber industries also contribute to the killing of bears and the destruction of their environment. Bears are viewed as a threat to cattle, sheep, and property, which supposedly justifies the slaughter. The fact is that bears usually avoid areas frequented by humans, but the prevailing opinion that bears are a menace is used as an excuse for excessive shooting, and is the main reason for the decline of the grizzly bear population. As humans move in and destroy the bear's natural habitat, the bears react by fleeing to new areas—but there are few places that a man with a gun is unable to reach. Even today, the black market is paying $75 an ounce for a bear's gall bladder on the mistaken assumption that it increases the human sex drive.

Despite the threat that humans pose to bears, they continue to thrive throughout the world; grizzlies live in Russia, Europe, Asia, and North America. There is a wide degree of error in the official estimates of current world bear populations because the bear census is based on estimates of wardens who fly over natural areas and count the number of bears they see. The black bear population of British Columbia is estimated at 120,000, and the grizzly population at 13,000. But there is little doubt that the overall population has been decreasing with the expansion of urban centres and the encroachment of natural areas by humans. I have travelled from New Brunswick to the Yukon, Northwest Territories, Hudson Bay, Alaska, British Columbia, and Alberta in order to study bears in their natural environment; my investigations led me to conclude that these animals are widely misunderstood.

My interest in bears began developing into a career when, in 1967, I started recording their activities on 16-mm film and colour slides and preparing a bear safety program. Every year, I speak to students at about 150 schools, not only about bears but also about the importance of respecting nature. I believe that describing my own experiences is the best way to educate young people and adults about animals and the environment.

As a result of my activities at the Jasper Park Lodge, people in the area began referring to me as the "bear man." The name stuck and followed me back to New Brunswick to the extent that children who have seen my slides and listened to my talks don't call me by any other name.

I have noted that wardens, rangers, and other park officials do not like the idea of me hiking in areas within their jurisdiction where bears are prevalent, and have tried several times over the years to prevent me from doing so. Although I understand their concern, I feel it is often unwarranted—by being cautious, one can minimize the risk of hiking in "bear country." This does not mean I would advise others to take the same risk, but I believe that observing bears at close quarters is the best way to understand them.

Over the past few years, I have been charged by grizzlies and black bears, and have even had a close call with a polar bear. Despite these incidents, I do not carry a gun or any other form of protection. If I am ever injured or killed by a bear, I urge those in authority not to blame the bear, for I take full responsibility for the risk I assume in studying bears as closely as I do. To me, the risk is an acceptable one: I hope not only to continue learning about bears and sharing my knowledge with others, but also to reduce the risk of a confrontation between bears and humans by developing precautions that, if heeded, will greatly reduce the chance of injuries resulting from bear attacks. This book will outline effective methods to avoid bear encounters and bear attacks, but first I would like to discuss the different types of bears and their habitats, and describe some of my experiences with bears, which have enabled me to develop some rules of bear safety.

The Bears I Know Best

There are seven species of bears.

The spectacled bears are the only bears that live in the southern hemisphere. They got their name from the white fur around their eyes. Because they live in warm temperatures their coat of fur is thin and since they have a source of food available year-round, they do not hibernate. They are good climbers and have longer legs than other bears. In its home in Equador, the bear climbs tall trees and feeds mainly on pambili palm.

The Asian black bear is found in Japan and westward to Iran. Its coat is charcoal black with a white v-shaped mark on its neck. When standing they are about 1.5 metres tall. Smaller than other bears, they stay in the Himalaya Mountains during the winter and climb to high elevations during the summer.

American black bears can be mostly charcoal black, brown, or white. These white black bears are found along the northern coast of British Columbia in Canada. White people call them "Kermodes" while native people call them "spirit bears" or "ghost bears."

Black bears live in the forests of central Asia and North America. They stand about 1.5 metres tall and normally don't weigh more than 225 kilograms. In Canada black bears are found in every province and territory except Prince Edward Island. In the United States they are found in every state except Kansas, Nebraska, Nevada, North Dakota, Connecticut, Delaware, Illinois, Indiana, Iowa, Maryland, and Rhode Island. There is a healthy population of black bears in the states of Washington, California, and Alaska. In Canada there is a large population of black bears in Ontario, Manitoba, Alberta, the Yukon Territory, and British Columbia.

Sloth bears live in Sri Lanka and India. They travel at night feeding mainly on insects and fruit. These bears have long fur and very long claws.

Often the cubs ride on their mother's back. All other bears have forty-two teeth except the sloth bear which has only forty.

The sun bear lives in Indonesia, Malaysia, Thailand, and Burma. Its name comes from the yellow patch on its chest, and compared with other bears its fur coat is very smooth which gives it a shiny appearance. Sun bears have a long tongue that enables them to eat insects and fruit quite easily.

Grizzly bears are found in Russia, northern Asia, Scandinavia, Spain, Canada, and the United States. At one time grizzlies lived in many parts of Europe, in Mexico, and in the state of California. But humans have completely exterminated them from Mexico, California, and most of Europe. In the lower forty-eight American states grizzly bears can be found only in Montana, Wyoming, and Idaho. The state of Alaska still has a healthy population of grizzly bears. In Canada, grizzly bears live in the provinces of Alberta and British Columbia, and both the Yukon and Northwest Territories have a healthy population of grizzlies living there.

Grizzly bears can be many colours: black, brown, silver-tipped, and a cream colour. The largest grizzly bears are found on Kodiak Island in Alaska. The main reason for this is these bears eat a very rich diet of spawning salmon—grizzlies have been known to weigh as much as 675 kilograms.

Polar bears live all over the Arctic Ocean and on the polar ice caps. Some have been known to travel south of the Arctic on ice floes and icebergs. During the winter their fur is pure white, but in the springtime it turns a creamy yellow. This colour blends in perfectly with the melting ice. Living in an area of ice and snow for nine to ten months of the year, polar bears are flesh-eating animals. Their main sources of food are ringed seals, bearded seals, walrus, guillemots, and other birds. They also feed on berries, lichen, and seaweed.

Being at home on the ice, in the water, and along the shoreline, their bodies are streamlined for swimming and running quickly. The back part of their body is higher, which enables them to run faster. Their neck is longer than other bears, and this enables them to swim great distances. Their beautiful white fur is very thick, keeping them warm during the freezing arctic winters, and is also an excellent camouflage when hunting and stalking prey. Polar bears listen for sounds of seals under the ice then dig them up with their front claws. They will also wait by a seal's breathing hole for long periods of time (three to four hours). When a seal appears the bear pulls it through the hole.

All bears have certain characteristics in common, some of which contradict popular notions about their habits and their nature. Their eyesight, for example, is often extremely keen; although bears can't always make out a stationary object, they can easily detect movement. Another widely-held misconception is that bears are slow and awkward; yet another, that they can't climb trees. In fact, bears are remarkably agile and can attain speeds of up to fifty kilometres per hour. All of them can get up a tree, even grizzlies (as I'll confirm in one of my accounts of a personal encounter with one of these massive animals), and many bears routinely climb trees as a reaction to possible danger.

Black bear eating soopalie berries.

As most people *do* know, bears eat just about everything, although some lean more towards a vegetarian diet, while others, such as polar bears, are primarily carnivorous. They all go through a period of hibernation, during which females—which are called sows—give birth to their cubs. Strongly territorial animals, they tend to be solitary rather than social and follow a hierarchy in which a smaller, weaker bear will usually yield to a more powerful one. A notable exception is a sow with cubs: a mother bear will fight even a much larger male—called a boar—with such tenacity that most bears give nursing sows a wide berth.

Cubs, which are born tiny and defenceless, live with their mothers for as long as three years, although eighteen months is more common. The mortality rate among young bears is quite high, but those that reach maturity can expect to live well into their teens and even reach the grand old age of thirty depending, of course, on the behaviour of their greatest natural enemy—humans.

There are, however, many differences among different varieties of bears. Here are three sketches of the bears I have encountered, and sometimes been lucky enough to film and photograph, during my years of hiking in wilderness areas from New Brunswick to Alaska.

Black Bears

The black bear is a massive, bulky animal that can grow to 1.5 metres in length and attain a shoulder height of up to 1.2 metres. Because it is such a large animal, many people assume the black bear is also extremely heavy. However, a sow often weighs as little as 68 kilograms and rarely more than 90 kilograms, while a boar, usually a bit heavier than a female black bear, averages between 110 kilograms and 135 kilograms. Several exceptionally large black bears have been sighted including a large boar that was caught and temporarily tranquillized in Riding Mountain Park, Manitoba. Before releasing the bear, the wardens weighed him and were astonished to find he weighed 360 kilograms.

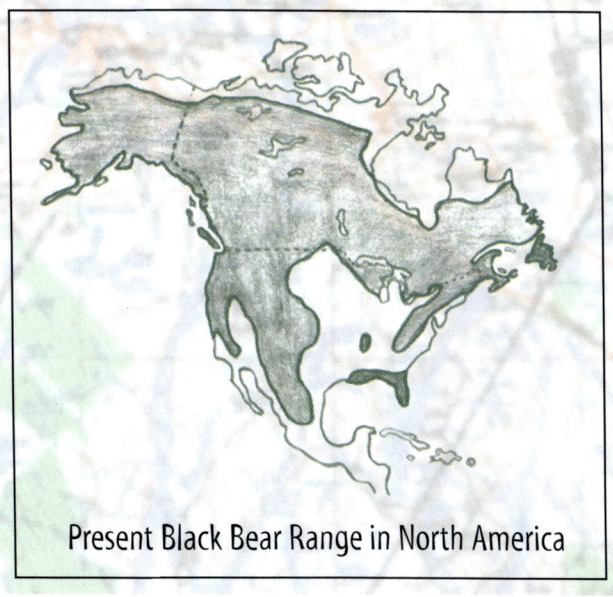
Present Black Bear Range in North America

Black bears are usually charcoal black, often with a white patch of fur on the chest. They can also be cinnamon, brown, white, and, rarely, black with a bluish tinge. The white bears, whose colour is a result of natural pigmentation—not the deficiency that produces albinos—live in British Columbia, while cinnamon-coloured black bears are most commonly found in the Rocky Mountains and to the west of that region.

Black bears are characterized by a straight profile, a tapered, sensitive nose, and long nostrils that come in very handy when the bear is browsing for food such as ants and small berries. Black bears have an extremely well developed sense of smell, better than that of human beings. They often stand on their hind legs and sniff the air for any unusual or attractive odours; black bears have been known to detect the scent of a dead animal from two kilometres away, and if the breeze is blowing in the right direction, they can smell a campfire from as far away as four kilometres. Hikers would be well advised to keep this in mind when choosing a site for the evening.

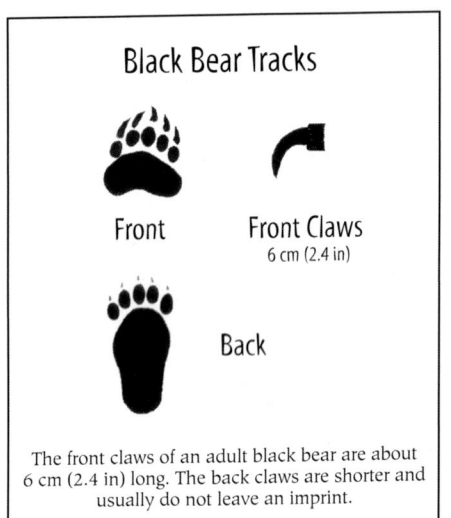

The front claws of an adult black bear are about 6 cm (2.4 in) long. The back claws are shorter and usually do not leave an imprint.

It has always been suggested that black bears have very poor eyesight; this is a myth. My experience indicates that bears can easily detect movement. It is true that they have difficulty making out a stationary object—if a distant observer remains motionless, the bear will usually continue what it is doing. But a bear that senses motion will approach the source of the movement, out of curiosity.

Sounds are an entirely different manner. Even a slight noise will alert a black bear to the position of an animal or person; the bear's large, round ears are well developed and extremely sensitive. This is why wearing "bear bells" is a popular way of reducing the risk of a chance encounter with a bear—and hikers who find themselves near a stream or a river are advised to sing or talk loudly as well as wearing the bells. If a bear hears the annoying bells or the loud talk, it is likely to leave the area, being as disinclined to meet up with a human as vice versa.

Despite their bulky appearance, black bears are both agile and quick. They may appear to be clumsily shuffling their feet when they move, but they are far from awkward and can, if need be, run as quickly as fifty kilometres an hour—which makes running from a bear a rather futile exercise. Like people, black bears—all bears, in fact—walk with the heel and sole of their feet touching the ground. Black bears have curved claws at the end of their feet, providing them with better traction and enabling them to dig up roots, remove bark from trees, and tear rotting trees apart as they search for insects.

Black bears are excellent climbers, and often clamber up a tree if they are scared or nervous. Inexperienced black bear cubs sometimes attempt to jump off a tree when they are close to the ground. A mother bear who senses danger chases her cubs up a tree, then sits at the bottom to protect them. When they climb, the bears grasp the tree with their front paws, then push themselves up by thrusting their hind legs forward; on their way down, they travel backwards, hanging on with their claws. Because black bears don't hesitate to climb trees, hikers should realize that they can't escape by going that route.

Black bear climbing tree.

Jumping in a lake is no better a solution. Black bears are excellent swimmers and can make it across a lake or river, provided there is some incentive on the opposite side. They even swim for fun, especially to cool off on a hot day. Because bears enjoy the water, it follows that one of their favourite foods is fish, which they catch with great skill, usually sticking to the shallow areas of lakes or streams, where their prey is much more accessible.

Black bears will eat almost anything, but vegetation forms the largest part of their diet. They also eat almost all berries, nuts, insects, fish, small animals, birds, bird's eggs, honey, and grass.

Black bears are exceptionally quiet animals; hikers only rarely hear them. But there are exceptions, such as the two bears I encountered in southeastern Alaska. These bears were apparently having a dispute over a fishing spot. They had been fishing peacefully a short distance apart, then suddenly noticed each other, came closer and began to growl and grunt

Black bear feeding on dandelions.

loudly for about four minutes. These sounds normally suggest a certain amount of annoyance on both sides—although in this case no fight broke out.

Bears also use sounds to convey danger. A sow may make a deep "whoof" sound or a whimpering noise if she is concerned for the safety of her cubs, which respond by promptly coming to her side. Black bears that find themselves in trouble make a sound remarkably similar to that of a baby crying.

Black bears mating.

In the fall, black bears react to cooler temperatures and shorter days by searching for a den and preparing for hibernation. Depending on the terrain, the den of choice could be a hollow tree, or a hole under a tree stump; some bears even make a crude den by covering themselves up with fallen leaves. Female black bears typically line their den with leaves or other green foliage, while the males, which take to their dens much later, often begin to hibernate only after the first snowfall.

There is a correlation between the number of winter months and the length of time a bear stays in its den. Black bears that live in the far north stay in their dens for five or six months, but those farther south emerge much sooner. In Mexico, black bears sleep for only a few days, and some do not hibernate at all. A bear in its den can be awakened by a distracting noise or a period of warm weather; the bear may even wander around outside the den for a while if temperatures are particularly high but then go back to sleep when the weather turns cold again.

Bears live within a very small area—usually no more than thirty kilometres—within which they develop routes that they use for

Black bear sow with two cubs.

travelling. Bears are most active early in the evening, during the night, and early in the morning.

With the exception of mating season, black bears are solitary animals and travel alone. At three years of age they attain sexual maturity and actively seek out a mate during the months of June and July.

Female bears give birth in the den, usually in January or early February. At birth, black bear cubs are toothless and hairless, and weigh less than one kilogram. Just after birth, the newborn cubs suckle for nourishment. Usually two cubs are born, but I have occasionally seen as many as four cubs.

During its first year of life, a newborn cub experiences rapid growth, reaching a weight of twenty-two kilograms by the time it is one year old. While cubs are still small enough to be extremely vulnerable, male black bears occasionally try to kill them for food; this is why sows make every attempt to keep boars away from their young. Boars are well aware of the tenacity of sows—that they are prepared to fight to the death to protect their cubs—and usually give them plenty of room.

A mother black bear looks after her cubs until they are about eighteen months old, at which point she either chases them away or she forces them up a tree and leaves the area. Eventually, the abandoned bears become hungry, begin to search for food and gradually learn to take care of themselves. Black bears can live as long as thirty years, but they do not usually last that long mainly because of their two most dangerous natural enemies—hunters and grizzly bears.

The black bear is a beautiful animal but is best observed and appreciated from a safe distance.

Grizzly Bears

Perhaps one of the most important things to know about grizzlies is that they are endangered in many parts of the world. Humans are responsible for this decline: hunting and encroaching on the bear's habitat has, for example, eliminated the grizzly population on the Canadian prairies. Because grizzlies have received a great deal of negative press, many people ignore the plight of these animals. My investigations have revealed that most of the negative attitudes to these bears are unwarranted. People do not have the right to destroy animals because they have developed biases against them; we must promote policies that will reverse this trend so that we can continue to enjoy these magnificent creatures.

Shaggy grizzly.

Grizzly bears live in a wide variety of areas—mountainous and coastal—throughout North America. Inland grizzlies inhabit three mountain zones: montane zone (valleys), subalpine zone (halfway up mountains), and alpine zone (mountain tops), while coastal bears are found throughout the Pacific Northwest and on Kodiak Island, Alaska.

Because of the range of environments in which grizzlies are found, the bears vary greatly in size and colour. But there are certain general characteristics. One quick way to distinguish between a black bear and a grizzly is that a grizzly has a pronounced hump on its shoulder. A grizzly's front claws are long and prominent, its body hair is long and coarse, and it has a small tail which often goes unnoticed. The hair of a grizzly can be black, dark brown, light brown, grey, or pale yellow. The ends of the hairs are sometimes white or silver, and such a bear is referred to as a silver-tipped grizzly. Grizzly hair can grow as long as ten centimetres; the lush fur coat provides insulation during the winter and helps keep the heat out during the hottest months. Towards late spring, a grizzly sheds its fur and begins growing a new coat. Bears stay cool in summer by choosing cool mountainous areas, swimming and resting in the shade.

Grizzlies located along the northwest coast are often called brown bears, because they are light or dark brown; the term Kodiak bear is used only in reference to a grizzly found on Kodiak Island. Kodiak bears are usually brown, but some can be black or silver-tipped. They are also the largest grizzlies, some weighing in at more than 680 kilograms and reaching just over three metres in length. The "rule of thumb" seems to be that enormous grizzlies are more commonly found in areas within eighty kilometres of the sea; Kodiak bears are extraordinarily large because they can catch salmon more than five months of the year.

Grizzly bear.

Pacific coast grizzlies, too, can grow to an impressive size—more than 360 kilograms and a little under three metres long—on a diet of salmon that can last as long as five months a year. However, inland grizzlies, which are mainly vegetarian, usually weigh less than 225 kilograms and grow to two metres in length.

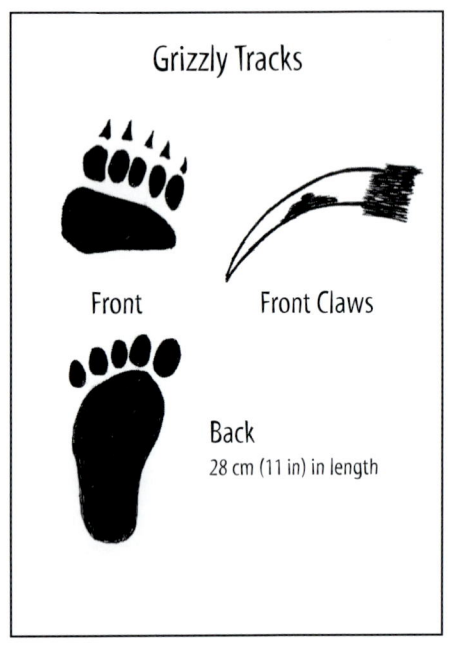

Front

Front Claws

Back
28 cm (11 in) in length

The teeth of a grizzly.

As their fishing ability suggests, grizzlies are excellent swimmers and, as I will later explain, at least one adult grizzly I know of is a good tree-climber. Grizzly cubs typically excel at both swimming and climbing, but during the second year of a cub's life, the front claws lose their curved shape, inhibiting the grizzly's ability to climb trees.

A grizzly's front claws—five on each foot—can grow to be more than six centimetres long, allowing the bear to delicately pluck berries from trees or dig for tubers and burrowing rodents. Excessive digging causes the claws to become short and blunt, but during the inactive months of the winter, their sharpness is restored. This pattern is repeated throughout the life of the bear.

A grizzly bear normally has forty-two teeth, which can grow as long as six centimetres. The back teeth have large crushing surfaces that are better for eating plants than meat. Indeed, even though the front teeth are sharp, the overall structure of a grizzly's mouth is more suited to a herbivorous diet. But grizzlies, like all bears, are omnivorous. The availability of food often determines a bear's diet. While their teeth are especially suited for vegetarian fare, they are by no means restricted to vegetables. Instinctively, bears want to vary their diet with meat.

It is just as much of a myth that grizzlies have poor eyesight as it is that any bear has trouble seeing. Their eyes are very small, but they function very well: grizzlies are able to detect moving objects in the distance and tend to investigate any unusual activity. On the other hand, if something far away remains still, the bear will have difficulty determining what it is, and will likely ignore it. As well as good eyesight, grizzlies have acute hearing, and any unusual sounds will draw their attention.

A grizzly's sensitive sniffer.

Grizzlies also have an excellent sense of smell because of their very large mucous membranes. A grizzly's sense of smell is seventy-five times keener than that of a human being. This ability is extremely useful in detecting either predators or prey. When a grizzly travels, it will often keep its nose close to the ground and continually sniff the air; even a whiff of something out of the ordinary will prompt a closer look.

A walking grizzly often appears awkward, but this is not the case. If prompted, a running grizzly will use light, bounding gallops and, like the black bear, can move as

Like humans, all bears walk with the sole and heels of their feet touching the ground.

Grizzly cubs wary of a nearby bear.

Montane zone.

quickly as fifty kilometres per hour. However, a bear running downhill slows up considerably to assure its footing.

The social structure of grizzlies is based on hierarchy within an independent way of life; bears are far from communal. Indeed, they are extremely protective of the area in which they live—their territory—and will chase away any intruder.

A sow's territorial range covers about 87 kilometres; if she has cubs, she drastically curtails her travelling—and, as a result, her territorial range. A boar's territorial range is about 120 kilometres, and this area expands during mating season as the male grizzly travels farther afield in search of a potential mate.

The bigger the bear, the more influence it commands; a smaller bear almost always yields to the larger without a fight. Interaction among grizzlies also involves a communication system—making a series of grunting noises, marking territories with their droppings, or leaving scratch marks on trees on the ground—that reduces the possibility of hostilities between the bears.

Sometimes these efforts to ensure privacy coincide with other needs. Grizzlies have to contend with a large population of mosquitoes; to deal with these flying pests, they rub up against trees until they are covered with sap, which acts as a natural insect repellent. But the practice offers a second benefit—in rubbing against a tree, they leave their scent behind. If another bear comes near and smells a fellow grizzly, it will leave the area.

The territories of some grizzlies overlap, which can result in an inadvertent meeting of the two bears. If this occurs, the larger bear gives chase, sometimes for quite a distance; I have seen these chases go as far as three kilometres. The smaller bear usually retreats to its home territory and will not be likely to "visit" the other grizzly again. If there are many grizzlies living in a relatively small area, the bears cut back on the size of their territories in an attempt to avoid encountering each other and tend to be more tolerant of the presence of interlopers.

Subalpine zone.

Nevertheless, confrontations do occur. A sow with cubs will not tolerate a male bear anywhere near her young bears because of the threat they may pose to her young: boars will kill and eat grizzly cubs. All the rules of hierarchy are forgotten when a boar approaches a mother grizzly: no matter how big he is, she will drive him away from the area and even fight him if necessary.

Alpine zone.

The diet of grizzly bears varies widely, depending on which of the three mountain zones they are inhabiting at any given time. First, a brief description of each. The montane zone is located below two thousand metres and usually encompasses valleys and forests. There are many varieties of foliage, including several kinds of berry bushes.

The subalpine zone begins near the thirteen-hundred-metre mark. This area is characterized by its many meadows and trees, and by a harsh climate, heavy rain and snowfalls.

The alpine zone is the area above two thousand metres. Very few trees grow in this area, but there is a vast array of flowers, including Indian paintbrush, mountain heather, and forget-me-nots; the alpine zone often resembles a spectacular living bouquet.

Grizzly eating grass.

While certain foods can be found in all three areas, such delicacies as berries are much more plentiful in the montane and subalpine zones, whereas squirrels—another favourite food—live in subalpine and alpine zones. Although larger animals can be found in all three zones, the chances of spotting them are better at higher elevations.

In early spring, grizzlies travel along mountain slopes, feeding on clovers, yellow bells, and spring beauties. Their bounteous springtime diet also includes grass, frogs, fish, willow catkins, aspen leaves, glacier lily bulbs, cow parsnip stems, hedysarum roots, alpinum roots, and carrion roots. The bears will also hunt for newborn deer, or seek out dead animals that may have been killed during a winter snowslide. Occasionally, a grizzly will strip the bark off of a tree and eat the juicy pulp.

The summer menu is very similar to the spring version, but there are a few scrumptious additions—shrubs, herbs, wasps, honey, frogs, insects, scats, birds, eggs, burrowing rodents, marmots, dry bear berries, and soopalie berries. Grizzlies enjoy these berries tremendously, despite their sourness, and they are abundant around the middle of July. When the berry crop is poor, bears eat more roots. Hedysarum roots, rich in both protein and minerals, are particularly sought after by bears because they are available most of the year.

The fall foods for grizzly bears include berries, roots, carrion, grass, squirrels, nuts, hedysarum roots, and fish. As the berries disappear,

Grizzly eating salmon.

grizzlies compensate by increasing their intake of roots and hunting squirrels more frequently.

Inland grizzlies are usually 85 per cent vegetarian, while coastal bears include plenty of fish in their diet. Grizzlies that live near salmon streams eat as much as sixteen kilograms of fish a day—and they enjoy just about every kind of salmon: pink, sockeye, coho, silver, and chinook.

Come September, grizzlies spend less time in the alpine meadows, where the already thick snow prevents them from reaching grasses, roots, and squirrels. Squirrels and marmots are also very inactive at this time of year, and this makes it even more difficult for a hungry bear to locate them. Bears now look hard for food, often travelling considerable distances to the subalpine and montane zones below, where the territory will remain snow-free for some time yet. There, grizzlies concentrate on eating fish, grass, roots, and the occasional squirrel.

By the end of October or early November, as temperatures plummet, the entire montane and subalpine zones are covered with snow. Roots and grasses are now inaccessible, and the grizzlies, unable to search for food, make ready for their winter sleep. They travel to the alpine or subalpine zones and search for a suitable spot to dig a den, which ideally will be located at an angle of about thirty to forty degrees beneath a canopy of small trees and roots. After finding an appropriate site, grizzlies dig themselves a small cave that will serve as their winter home. Bears are far from claustrophobic; indeed, bear dens are usually cramped—hardly big enough to crawl in and out. Some bears make their dens cozier by lining them with grass and leaves.

Grizzly bear's den.

During the hibernation period the grizzly's heartbeat slows down, and the bear's energy requirements decrease. The surplus fat built up during the summer and fall will keep them alive all winter; bears can sleep as long as six months without needing to eat. The extra fat also acts as a large blanket, keeping the bear warm as it sleeps.

The winter sleep, although long, differs from a typical hibernation, in which bears remain motionless. Grizzlies do move around occasionally during the winter; however, the bears do not wake up until warm weather arrives or unless they are disturbed. Much like humans, bears toss and turn when asleep, and the sound of an avalanche or any loud noise near the den will wake a hibernating bear. Residents of Kodiak Island have reported seeing bears roaming around all winter long, but this is unusual. Boars and sows without cubs hibernate alone and usually do not leave their dens until springtime—the end of April or early in May. However, they have been seen emerging from their winter dwellings as early as February or March.

During the winter months, grizzlies lose about 10 per cent of their body weight, so finding food is a priority. But the abundance of spring makes this an easy task, and the bear's lost weight is quickly regained as the yearly cycle begins once again.

Grizzlies become sexually active between the ages of three and five and are considered sexually mature when they are five years old. During the mating season, which occurs in late May and throughout June, boars are able to locate female bears by using their excellent sense of smell. When a boar finds a possible mate, an unusual ritual begins. First, the sow acts nervously in the presence of the boar and runs away—only to return and charge the boar. Next, the two bears become playful and begin nuzzling each other. Finally, the bears will become intimate. After the two bears have mated, they lose interest in each another and go their separate ways in search of another mate. In other words, both the male and female bears are promiscuous!

A grizzly asleep in its den.

The gestation period for grizzlies is about 255 days. A sow usually gives birth to as many as three cubs every four or five years but occasionally has four cubs at once. Grizzly cubs are born either in January or February, during their mother's hibernation. At birth, grizzlies are toothless, hairless, and unable to open their eyes; they weigh less than half a kilogram and rely entirely on their mother to survive, nursing from her and cuddling with her for warmth. During hibernation, both mother and cubs survive on the excess body fat that the mother has accumulated before entering her den. Accordingly, grizzly cubs survive with very little nourishment during the first few months of their lives.

For more than a year, grizzly cubs nurse on their mothers' milk, which is extremely rich—about 30 per cent fat. While nursing, the cubs follow the mother bear and eat the same foods she does. A year-old grizzly has begun eating grasses, roots, berries, fish, and carrion, imitating its mother and gradually learning to seek out food for itself.

Cubs stay with their mother for two and a half years, sometimes three years, if the sow has not yet found another mate. By that age, the cubs have learned what to eat, where to find food, where to dig a den, and how to hunt. The young bears have also found out how to recognize danger and respond appropriately. As the learning period ends, the bear cubs and their mother soon eat farther apart; they may become permanently separated during that time or the sow may eventually chase the cubs away. Either by chance or by choice, mother and cubs finally go their separate ways; the mother bear seeks out a boar, and the mating process starts again. The mortality rate for young bears is extremely high; as many as four in ten grizzlies have been known to live as long as thirty years, but a life span in the high teens or low twenties is more common.

Negative attitudes towards grizzlies are unwarranted and usually supported by those who like to kill for "sport," or some perverse sense of power. If there were no restrictions on killing bears, they would be extinct today. Of the men I've met who have shot bears, they consider themselves heroes for shooting a defenceless animal.

Polar Bears

The polar bear can only be found in arctic regions and differs considerably from black bears or grizzlies due to its unusually harsh environment. Polar bears have adapted their feeding and hunting habits both physically and behaviourally in response to the low temperatures and rugged landscape of their northern habitat.

These bears are able to travel extremely long distances, and have been known to follow seal herds for almost two thousand kilometres. Other journeys begin quite by accident: occasionally, a polar bear inadvertently hitches a ride on an iceberg and ends up floating as far south as Newfoundland. The bears would probably remain in their new environment, at least for a while; but they are always rounded up by some meddlesome human, tranquillized and transported back north.

Polar bears vary in size, with some males weighing as much as 675 kilograms. A more common weight is about 360 kilograms for boars and considerably less than that for the smaller female bears. They have beautiful fur that can range from pale yellow to pure white, but the nose and most of the face is black. The skulls and necks of polar bears are longer than those of other bears, producing the characteristically prominent frontal area. Their claws are short and sharp—ideal implements for holding food.

Polar bear.

The teeth of polar bears are very sharp and shaped to shear meat, which forms 90 per cent of their diet. Their usual prey is the ringed seal; however, they also hunt bearded, harp, and hooded seals. Ringed seals can weigh as much as sixty-eight kilograms—a gargantuan meal, to say the least! Polar bears hunt seals by first waiting patiently near blowholes in the arctic ice, where seals come up to breathe. As a seal emerges, the bear will strike with its sharp claws, then use its powerful jaws to drag the seal out of the water and onto the ice, where the bear's meal begins almost immediately.

Polar bears also hunt seals by creeping up on them as they doze on the ice. A bear will first search for a sleeping seal then slowly approach; about thirty metres away, the skilled hunter rushes forward with long bounding jumps, trying to get between the seal and the only possible escape—the blowhole. The seal heads for the hole, but unless it is having a very lucky day, it is destined to become lunch—or dinner, as the case may be. When polar bears are extremely hungry, they will eat the bones as well as the meat, blubber, and skin. Usually, however, bears will only eat a small portion of a seal.

Male polar bears are dominant in the polar bear hierarchy; however, if a female polar bear with cubs is nearby, no males will approach. As with all bears, they are extremely protective of their young and do not hesitate to chase away or fight larger males that may pose a threat.

Polar bears become sexually active between four to five years of age. The mating season begins in April. During this time, male and female polar bears stay in one location for up to several weeks. The sow may have cubs, but this has no effect on her desire to mate.

When a female polar bear becomes pregnant, she leaves the arctic ice and travels to land. There, the search along the shoreline begins for a suitable spot to build a den, usually a cave dug in a snowdrift or in a snowbank, ideally located along a hillside. In the James Bay and Hudson Bay areas, pregnant polar bears will travel farther inland, often until they reach trees. There, a bear will dig a den in dirt or gravel on the side of a hill.

Polar bears are born in the mother's den during December or January. Litters normally consist of either one or two cubs, although, on rare occasions as many as three are born. At birth, like other bears, the cubs are toothless and hairless, they are unable to see, and they weigh less than a kilogram. These delicate creatures depend on their mother to provide sustenance and warmth; they nurse on her milk until they leave the den in March.

Once out in the "real world," the education of young polar bears begins, as they imitate the behaviour of their mother. When the cubs are a year old, the mother polar bear is still sharing her food with them, but they are learning how to hunt. The cubs stay with their mother for two and a half years, after which the young bears are left on their own. This is a dangerous time for them, because they are extremely curious and will investigate any nearby noise. Bears that inadvertently approach hunters are making an unfortunate and usually fatal mistake.

As the human population increases in the Arctic, the numbers of polar bears will certainly decline. It is up to all of us to preserve the fragile Arctic environment that supports this playful, strong, and majestic animal.

2

Hiking in New Brunswick

Southern NEW BRUNSWICK

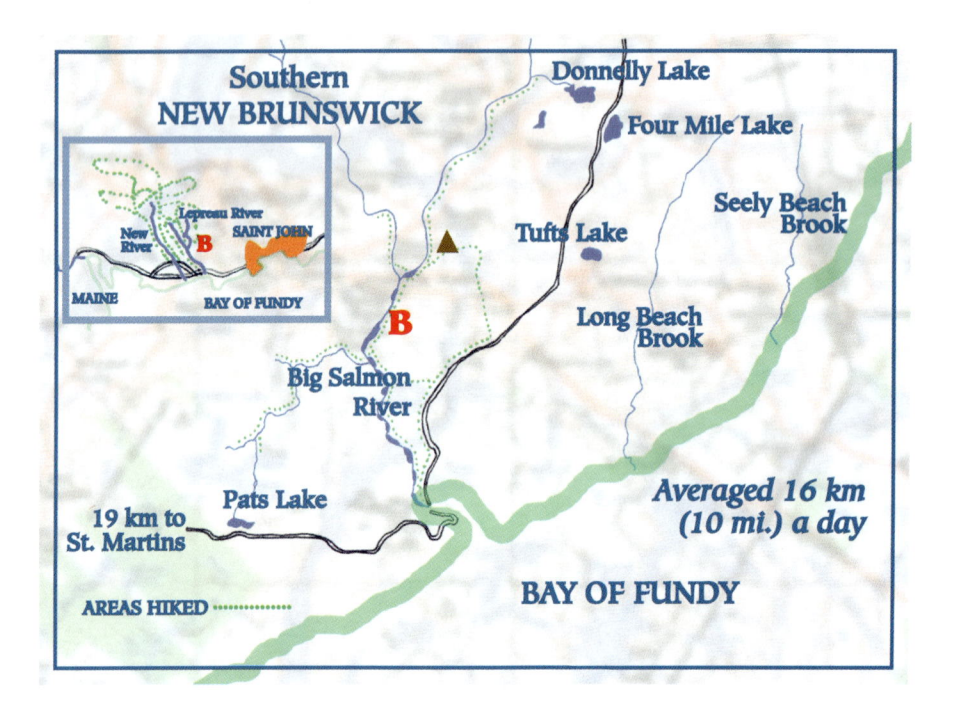

Donnelly Lake
Four Mile Lake
Seely Beach Brook
Tufts Lake
Long Beach Brook
Leprosu River
SAINT JOHN
New River
MAINE
BAY OF FUNDY
Big Salmon River
Pats Lake
19 km to St. Martins
Averaged 16 km (10 mi.) a day
BAY OF FUNDY
AREAS HIKED ············

The Maritimes are not renowned for their bear populations, but there are black bears in areas of New Brunswick, Newfoundland, and Nova Scotia. There is an abundance of other wildlife such as deer, moose, squirrels, foxes, and porcupines, and the scenic beauty of this part of Canada is well known.

New Brunswick is particularly beautiful in the autumn—an ideal time to go hiking. Anyone unfamiliar with this part of Canada should be delighted with their first experience of the fall foliage—a kaleidoscope of reds, yellows, oranges, and browns mingled with the last traces of summer's green. To get a true feel for the outdoors, it may be necessary to venture fifteen kilometres or more into the woods, but even a leisurely drive will give you a taste of nature.

I spent most of my youth hiking in northern New Brunswick, either alone or with friends. Trout were plentiful in the main rivers in the area, and I often saw deer and moose but no sign of bears.

One of my favourite places to hike is near Lepreau, in southern New Brunswick, forty kilometres west of Saint John on the highway towards St. Stephen. The beauty and serenity of this area are remarkable.

On one of my trips there, I was hiking along the upper stretches of the New River deadwater on a balmy afternoon. New River is one of the many rivers in New Brunswick that flows into the Bay of Fundy. I was neither seeking nor expecting any excitement, so it came as quite a surprise when I looked down and realized that the distinctive imprints I saw in the mud were recent—and unmistakably those of a bear. I knew this was not a very large bear, as the tracks were only ten centimetres long, and because they had not yet dried, I felt my guard go up.

But all was quiet around me in the thick forest, and I convinced myself that the bear was undoubtedly gone. Besides, I was more concerned with catching a trout than seeing a bear, so I tossed my fishing line into the nearby pond. Everything was calm. The only disturbance was the occasional ripple caused by my fishing line. As usual, I was not having much luck catching fish, so I began to walk along the muddy shoreline toward the small stream that fed the deadwater.

Suddenly, there was a rustling in the thick bushes immediately to my left. I tensed, remembering the tracks I had seen earlier, and stood stock-still. I thought I saw the gaze of a shadowy figure in the bushes, and felt I was being watched, but by the time my eyes had adjusted to the shifting lights, whatever it was had vanished into the dense underbrush. I was shaken for a few moments, but later laughed at how my mind was playing tricks on me.

That night, I camped about half a mile from the deadwater. I was disappointed at not having caught any fish and decided to settle down early. Deep in the woods it can get very dark, and this was one of those moonless nights when a hiker without a flashlight can end up in big trouble. But I wasn't going anywhere till morning, and it was a calm night; what could happen? Reassured, I fell asleep.

I was jolted out of a sound sleep by a scraping noise that seemed to be coming from about two metres away, just outside my tent. I groped for my flashlight, but it was nowhere to be found. Uh-oh, trouble. This night was clearly not going well. My next line of defence was to begin talking aloud to myself; I began to express my love for all animals—especially bears. Soon the scratching sounds stopped. My voice may have succeeded in scaring the animal away; I could only guess that it was a bear, and I was most pleased not to have found out for certain what it was.

The hooting of owls soon broke the silence. It had all happened very quickly, and I was still shaking. I didn't sleep much that night, but I feel my insomnia was justified. I found myself wondering if the trip had been worth it: I had caught no fish, and I had nearly been killed by a giant bear. (First bear encounters—or, rather, *possible* first encounters—tend to be a little exaggerated.) From this experience I learned my first lesson in bear survival: take a flashlight when hiking in the woods, and have it close at hand when you retire for the night. Lesson two: when you think a bear is approaching, start talking because the sound of a human voice keeps animals away.

Big Salmon River.

Later that summer, my friend Dan Craig and I decided to go on a three-day camping trip and do some fishing on the Lepreau River, about sixteen kilometres east of New River. Dan was in my class at vocational school. He was a strong hiker and a good companion. We both carried a sleeping bag and matches, cutlery and a frying pan to cook our trout in, and a pot. Of course we also took our fishing rods, leaders, and trout flies. The flies and mosquitoes encouraged us to keep moving from one hole to another, and, before we knew it, we had covered about ten kilometres. Finally, a nice breeze in the late afternoon relieved us and we stopped at a promising fishing hole in hopes of adding to the three trout we had managed to catch.

No sooner had we cast our lines when, about twenty metres away, a large bear leapt out of the bushes and approached the riverbank. The bear, which was charcoal black and appeared to weigh about ninety kilograms, began to feed along the mossy shoreline. For the first few moments, he ignored us, and we tried to take advantage of this fortunate indifference by attempting to slowly back away into the woods. Our good fortune quickly ran out, however, as the bear caught a glimpse of our movements. It was one of those unforgettable moments: the bear stared at us, and all we could do was stare right back at him.

Dan and I had always taken for granted that we were safe in the woods; however, we had never anticipated coming face to face with a bear. Our inexperience—and our fear—soon got the better of us, and we took off at full steam through the woods. No matter what danger lay ahead, we were sure it could be no worse than the danger we were leaving behind. Certain that the bear was hot on our heels, I kept looking over my shoulder as we ran, fearing it would overtake us and chew us to death. We ran until fatigue overcame us and our adrenaline ran out. It was a comical moment, and Dan and I began to laugh at our "bravery." The gruesome bear stories we had heard as youngsters remained with us, evidently; we were not at all sure if the tales were true, but we did not want to find out. Still smiling at our extreme instinctive reaction, we started our hike out of the area.

As I look back on the incident, it occurs to me that Dan and I were very lucky that day. We did not react well to the situation: running from a bear only gets the animal excited, and this makes the predicament worse. We would have done much better to continue the slow retreat we began, instead of bolting because of panic. But we live and learn.

*****

Big Salmon River is located in a particularly rugged section of southern New Brunswick, about fifty-eight kilometres east of Saint John. Steep hills and cliffs are typical of the terrain, and there is an abundance of maple trees. The area is harsh, but at certain times of the year, it is beautiful. In spring, mayflowers and violets grow in abundance. Lady-slippers, trout lilies, and pitcher plants, their leaves often filled with water and captured flies, bloom in the swamps. As in many other parts of the province, the fall colours are outstanding, and the combination of bright red, orange, green, and yellow foliage against the stark background of the jutting hills makes for a spectacular visual feast.

The majestic Big Salmon River, with its crystal-clear waters, is a perfect complement to its surroundings. The river contains several deep pools, in which Atlantic salmon spawn each year—an irresistible appeal to a bear's appetite. The prevalence of this favourite food makes the Big Salmon River area quite a "hot spot" for bears; their only challenge is getting at their prey, which are often annoyingly out of reach in pools too deep for the bears to fish. But bears can be sneaky—a nice serving of salmon is theirs to enjoy should a fisherman leave his catch unattended. Or, since most fishermen clean their catches along the shore, the bears will at least be able to content themselves with munching on the entrails. In fact, these fish "insides" are a very attractive meal both for bears and other local wildlife.

I was introduced to the river in my early twenties and often returned to this scenic wonderland. During one of my recent October fishing visits I noticed a dark shadow moving along the shallow section of the river. The "shadow," a full-grown black bear, lumbered its way along the riverbank then went into the woods. I could tell it was an adult bear because its movements were slow and casual, and when I had a closer look at where it had been walking, I got the "inside story" on this bear's successful foraging expedition along the rocky shoreline.

A visit to the Big Salmon River area requires some caution, but for anyone who is feeling brave and is interested in seeing signs of bears, there is one sure-fire method. Simply locate one of the many overturned tree stumps covered with long, narrow grooves. These stumps have been overturned by bears pursuing a dessert of ants and other insects; the grooves are the marks left by their claws.

Big Salmon River, like many other rivers in New Brunswick, is rich in both scenic beauty and wildlife. Someday, I hope, the area will be made into a preserve, thus allowing the many animals and fish to continue surviving in this beautiful spot. If areas such as Big Salmon River were protected, not only would visitors have a natural area to observe wildlife, but the salmon stocks would be allowed to replenish themselves. Unless we become serious about protecting our animals, birds, and fish soon, there will be nothing left to protect and no wildlife for our children to see.

Banff National Park

Those who would like to experience nature at its finest should visit Banff National Park and Lake Louise, Alberta, sometime during their lives. The area possesses a compelling and powerful beauty; one's first glimpse of the Rocky Mountains makes it clear why Banff and Lake Louise have become two of the world's foremost tourist attractions.

Unfortunately, Banff and Lake Louise have lost some of their natural flavour due to excessive commercial development in recent years; in the battle between nature and industry, nature is often defeated. Nevertheless, the spectacular scenery warrants a visit. The village of Lake Louise is about an hour's drive from Banff, a breathtaking excursion well worth the trip.

The first time I saw the Rocky Mountains was in 1967 when I decided to venture out of New Brunswick for a new hiking experience. Once I saw the mountains and the abundance of bears, I became determined to make nature programs for schools to introduce children to the fascinations of the natural world. I lived in this area for several years, and my mother would frequently come out from New Brunswick to visit. One time, during a visit in 1972, she expressed a desire to see some bears. Dorothy Scott was a tough woman, but she had no idea what she was letting herself in for—and on this occasion, neither did I.

For many years the Lake Louise dump had been a popular gathering place for grizzly bears—and tourists. Throughout the spring, summer, and fall, bears would regularly show up to pick through the garbage, and visitors would show up to look at the bears. It was quite a spectacle; there were times when as many as twenty cars would line up at the dump for a glimpse of a grizzly. If my mother were going to see a bear on this trip, she would get her safest view from inside a car parked at the dump. Or so I believed.

The Rocky Mountains.

We arrived early, and about an hour before dark, the bears began to emerge from the woods and approach the dump. Within half an hour, seventeen grizzlies were in the vicinity of the dump. The biggest one was a boar that weighed close to 180 kilograms, unusually large for an inland bear. His great size marked him as the dominant bear in the group; wherever he went, the others gave him plenty of space.

Mom was having a great time watching this enormous creature, and we hardly noticed that darkness was approaching and the other cars were starting to leave. Finally, we were the only ones left. Time to go, we decided—but it was not to be. My old car just refused to start. The battery was dead, and my mother was certain that we soon would be, too. We waited for a car to come to our rescue, but nobody arrived.

The large bear, which I refer to as Godzilla, must have sensed how uncomfortable we were, because he decided to give us a closer inspection. First, he approached the car, then went directly to the passenger-side window and pressed his nose against the glass. Godzilla's nostrils were less than half a metre from my mother's, and it would be no understatement to say that she was wildly excited; however, this was not the sort of excitement one usually courts. All I could do was to feign an expressionless face as Godzilla casually rubbed his nose back and forth across the glass.

The car was silent except for the sniffing sounds on the other side of the window and the occasional agonized sigh from my mother. Upon reflection, I'm glad my mother didn't say anything, because I'm not sure that under the circumstances they would "bear" repeating.

Soon another bear came over for a look, and this one ambled over to the driver's side instead. My bravado vanished, and I was afraid there would soon be a puddle on my seat. I began visualizing a night in a dump with seventeen hungry bears, all with their faces pressed up against the car windows. I snapped out of my nightmare when I noticed a pair of headlights suddenly illuminate the entrance to the dump. The lights frightened the bears away, and after a boost from the much-welcomed Good Samaritan, we gratefully exited the dump.

Grizzlies head towards the Lake Louise dump.

Mom refused to let nature have the last word, so she insisted that we go on a hike soon afterward. Her only request: "Make sure this hike is easy—and bear-free." This was not a simple request: there is always some degree of difficulty—and risk—when hiking in the Rockies. Nevertheless, we went hiking; I chose one of the most beautiful and popular spots in the Rockies, the Columbia Ice Fields. There is a trail near the ice-field chalet, about three kilometres long, but well worth the effort because of the scenery; the view is one of the finest. The trail leads gradually uphill until it reaches a series of lush green meadows and a spectacular outlook onto one of the most beautiful views I have ever seen.

As we began to hike, I questioned whether I should have chosen an easier trail. After almost two kilometres of huffing and puffing, I got my answer when I asked Mom how she was doing. She glared at me and replied: "I have news for you. I couldn't go any farther up or down, unless it was to kill you—then maybe I could move." Despite her ruddy face and angry words, I could tell she really was enjoying herself; it was just going to take a while to convince her that she was having fun. After a short rest, we resumed our hike and were pleased to see several bighorn sheep and a coyote. Luckily, for me, we did not see any bears. Her sense of adventure was not spoiled, so I took her hiking at Portal Creek in Jasper National Park.

Shortly after the excursion, Mom went home to New Brunswick, saying she could "hardly wait" to do it all again. She did not visit me again for a long time, although I am sure she remembered the trip fondly.

My next journey, shortly after my mother's departure, was to the Cascade River, near Banff. I was hoping to get some good photographs of bears so I drove to the trailhead of the Cascade River to begin looking for a promising hiking area. Just off the highway, I noticed a side road blocked off by a fence. I parked my car and went over to have a closer look. Odd, I thought, a locked fence obstructing a road that appears to be very well maintained. Beyond the fence was a sign that read CASCADE FIRE ROAD—NO MOTOR VEHICLES ALLOWED BEYOND THIS POINT, N.P.C. That meant any driver entering the road would have to obtain a set of keys from National Parks Canada officials to unlock the fence.

Dorothy Scott hiking at Portal Creek.

Bighorn sheep near the Columbia Ice Fields.

I decided to hike in, and noticed quickly that the "closed" road was certainly attracting a lot of activity. In a short time, eleven vehicles passed me, including an RCMP car, six Parks Canada vehicles, and four private autos. It seemed pretty obvious to me that these vehicles had motors, so I surmised that whoever was in charge of enforcing the road closure was inclined to hand out a lot of keys to drivers wanting to go past that fence.

The sight of all those vehicles travelling on a closed road was, to me, just another example of how poorly the parks are managed. A national park must have as its first priority the preservation of natural areas. This "natural area" was more like a bustling urban highway.

To escape all the exhaust fumes, I took a short detour to the Cascade River. Soon I was hiking along a path parallel to the shoreline, where I noticed an abundance of soopalie berries. These berries are a delicacy for bears, and a large crop of them—especially ripe ones—can be an indicator of a prime bear area. Soopalie berries are orange and red when ripe; they grow on both short and tall bushes and are easy for hungry bears to reach.

Because the trail I was on led directly to these berries, I suspected that I had been hiking on a bear trail, a path worn into the forest floor by years of regular bear traffic. My suspicions were confirmed when, a few moments later, I noticed animal droppings speckled with whole soopalie berries. Some berries remain intact as they travel through a bear's digestive system; when I saw droppings that contained those berries, I knew a bear could be nearby—and that, in addition to soopalie berries, it had recently enjoyed a feast of squirrel, another staple of a bear's diet. I recognized the light-brown hairs intermixed with the droppings.

Soopalie berries.

My awareness heightened, I continued hiking, my camera at the ready, attached to a strap around my neck. Then I heard the familiar sound I had been anticipating—a deep, guttural "WHOOF." I froze. There it was, emerging from the swaying bushes about thirty metres in front of me—a bear with a hump on his back. This was a grizzly.

The bear was balancing on his hind legs, and from where I stood, he looked like a furry skyscraper. In fact, he was about as tall as I, but probably three times my weight: clearly, this grizzly had all the advantages. A grizzly on his hind legs, glaring into the camera, is quite an unusual image, although my shaking hands would make it difficult to take the perfect picture. Nevertheless, I tensed my trembling knees and snapped the shutter, rationalizing that a blurry photo was better than no photo at all. As I lowered the camera, the grizzly came down off his hind legs and began swaggering toward me. The key to survival in these situations is to remain calm; I had learned this after many close calls. One must always keep in mind that an excited bear is a dangerous bear; any sudden movements, for example, are likely to cause agitation—and this is never a good sign.

Keeping all of this in mind, I slowly and calmly backed up, then changed direction and kept walking until I thought I was out of harm's way. Out of the frying pan, into the fire: I had just retreated from one bear, and now, approaching me from the other direction, were two others. I knew these latest arrivals were relatively young bears, because they were much smaller than the first. But they were big enough just the same.

Whenever I find myself in this sort of situation, I simply begin talking to the bears.

Standing grizzly.

Padded-down bear trail.

Perhaps I continue to do this because it had the desired effect during my first encounters with bears, in New Brunswick—they always left. By this time, I had a vast catalogue of possible subjects, each guaranteed to charm a bear. Actually, I mention anything that comes into my mind that suits the occasion, for example, "I know this is your berry patch so I'll just back up slowly and you can have all the berries," or "Don't get excited, I'll get out of your way." On this occasion I professed my undying love of furry forest creatures, especially bears. It might have been wiser to begin talking to God. The bears were still coming, and they had advanced to within ten metres.

I decided to change my tactics and adopt a more vigorous approach. "I will get off the trail if you want me to," I called out in an indignant voice. I think the bears knew they had the upper hand—whether I was willing to concede this point or not—but they must have taken pity on me, because the lead bear suddenly veered to the left and the other followed. These grizzlies had evidently decided not to stoop to eating the likes of me when there were so many other delicacies in the area. Within about thirty seconds there was not a bear in sight. After recovering from my shock, I looked around for a place to pitch my tent and tried to settle down for the evening. It was difficult to sleep, but I finally managed to catch a few winks. It was more important for me to be out communing with nature than to give in to my fear and head for the nearest motel.

The next afternoon, while hiking on another nearby bear trail, I spotted a large grizzly lying in the shade. Bears enjoy the shade, which offers them relief from the intense heat. This was an ideal opportunity to snap a few quick pictures; approaching with caution and trying not to make any sudden movements, I hid behind a tree and got a few good shots. The grizzly turned its head in my direction, but it didn't get up. Back on the trail, I thought about the good luck I have had with bears over the years, and how my luck was certainly holding on this trip. Maybe luck was not the entire explanation though; some of the techniques I was developing in my behaviour around bears seemed to be proving effective.

As I made my way down the path, I once again encountered the Cascade River and crossed the bear trail again. On the opposite shore was a steep hill that had been carved by winter snowslides. Wide paths, which ran vertically up the hill, were beginning to be replenished with small trees

Cascade River and avalanche area.

and bushes. Such avalanche areas are often ideal vantage points for observing wildlife; in particular, bears that come in search of small animals living among the rocks, and, in this case, the soopalie berries springing up in large numbers amidst the new vegetation.

I wondered why it was that the best spots to see bears are always located on the other side of a freezing stream; then, after only a moment's hesitation, I took the plunge.

Crossing the river turned out to be an unwise decision, because once I reached the other side I was drenched and cold. As any experienced hiker can confirm, there is nothing worse than hiking in wet clothes—especially wet footwear. Hiking across rivers has been a mistake I have made many times, but I never seem to learn my lesson. So I decided to ignore the dampness and walk along another animal trail that ran parallel to the avalanche area.

I was hardly into my wet journey, when, suddenly, I was confronted with a mother bear, standing on her hind legs directly in front of me. Behind her stood a large cub. I knew this was a dangerous moment; a sow is very protective of her young and is prepared to chase anything that threatens her family.

My instincts told me this bear did not want to exchange pleasantries with an interloper such as myself—and that, indeed, she might consider making me part of her diet. With these unsettling thoughts in mind, I calmly turned, walked back to the water's edge and once again began the freezing-cold journey to the other side and safety. When I got to the centre of the stream, I glanced back to make sure the bears were not pursuing me. By then, the sow and cub were sitting beside the riverbank, watching my ungracious retreat. I will swear they had big smiles on their faces. I gave them an indignant glare and continued across.

My pride shaken but intact, I returned to the Cascade Fire Road and began the hike back to my car. On the road, I came upon several more vehicles, including a Parks Canada truck with two park wardens inside. I wanted to find out why there was so much traffic on what was supposed to be a closed road, so I stood directly in front of the truck.

The wardens slowed down and exchanged one of those "What now?" questioning looks. I approached the driver and stated matter-of-factly: "I'm placing you two under arrest. Give me your names." After complying with my request, the warden smiled and asked me what the charge was. I told him about the many vehicles I had encountered; if the road was going to have a sign saying that it was closed, I said, then it should be enforced. I went on to explain that by allowing vehicles on this road, they were ruining the valley; traffic and nature do not mix well. If nothing is done to inhibit traffic, I added, the road will eventually be used by all comers, and the natural area will be destroyed. I urged the wardens to consider permanently closing the road and turning it into a hiking trail. The warden listened indifferently to my environmental theories, then wordlessly drove away.

I argued for permanent closure of that road, because I have come to agree with the beliefs that a good friend of mine, Jim Kahl, has always expressed—if wilderness areas are to remain wild, they must be free of human intervention. Despite the commercial appearance of many parks, it is important to remember that they serve many purposes, one of the most important of which is preserving the environment within the park area. In Banff and Jasper the commercialization is far too pronounced.

For example, the Athabasca River, near Jasper, is polluted. Several mills that operate just outside the park use the river as a convenient dumping ground. Perhaps the waste is properly treated, as the operators of the mill might argue, but the impact of industry on the environment seems impossible to ignore when one considers that the Athabasca River, once filled with fish, is now almost empty. The question must be asked: what is the point in establishing a park if we are then going to let industry surround and destroy it?

I believe a proper and equitable balance between commercial interests and environmental protection should be the goal of Parks Canada. Thus far, it has not been met; instead, the balance of power has been on the side of commercial gain. And since nature is the underdog in the battle, every small victory—even closing down an unneeded road—is a step in the right direction.

Grizzly sow and cub.

Because the concerns I have frequently expressed over the years about a number of issues have been largely ignored, I am accustomed to being disappointed when I make a complaint. That is why I was pleasantly surprised on my next visit to the Cascade River, to find the Cascade Fire Road permanently blocked. The two vehicle bridges on the road had been replaced by smaller walking bridges. Indeed, the entire road had been converted into a hiking and horse trail. This time, thankfully, balance had been tipped in favour of nature.

Shortly after I parted company with the wardens in the Parks Canada truck, my travels took me to the beautiful Bow River, not far from Lake Louise. It was a sunny day and an ideal time to hike, so I unpacked my gear and prepared for a nice walk in this picturesque area. I began hiking along an animal trail, which eventually moved away from the river, towards some nearby hills where I hoped to see some animals and possibly get some good pictures. It soon became apparent to me that bears were the primary travellers on this particular animal trail. The evidence was everywhere. For example, the scratches and claw marks on many of the trees in the area were sure signs of young bears, which had tried to climb them by digging into the bark. My awareness heightened, I continued on.

Approaching grizzly.

Further along the trail, I saw a tree with strands of black bear fur clinging to the trunk. Bears occasionally rub against the bark of a tree to free themselves from insects that burrow into their fur. A tree used for this purpose is referred to—in my scientific vocabulary—as a "scratching-and-rubbing-tree." I have witnessed bears using these trees, and they contort their bodies into very strange positions indeed. After approaching the tree, the bear stands on its hind legs, then begins moving up, down, and sideways—seemingly all at the same time. Imagine a bear dancing with a tree; that's what it looks like.

An adult bear marks a scratching-and-rubbing-tree as its own by scratching it with his claws or by urinating on it, thus leaving a scent behind as a warning to other bears. Any interlopers who come across these signs will stay away from the area, knowing they have discovered another bear's rubbing tree.

As I walked, I noticed that the centre of the path was raised, while

Two grizzlies resting in the shade.

both outer edges were worn down. This occurs when bears use a trail frequently. Over time, the crushing weight of the bear thundering down on the ground erodes the outer edges and leaves a raised section in the centre of the trail. I did not have to go far before confirming my suspicions about bear activity in this area. About ten metres in front of me, two grizzlies—each easily weighing over one hundred kilograms—were lying in a shady area beside the trail.

 The bears did not notice me; they were looking in the opposite direction from where a third grizzly was approaching. Good grief! Three of them! I cautiously took some pictures, then slowly backed away. The bears turned and watched me leave, but my movements were slow enough not to excite them. Meeting three bears in the forest certainly raises your blood pressure, but getting a few good photos (and escaping) makes it all worth while. All the same, I had had enough excitement for one trip. Time to return to civilization.

42   *Hiking In Bear Country*

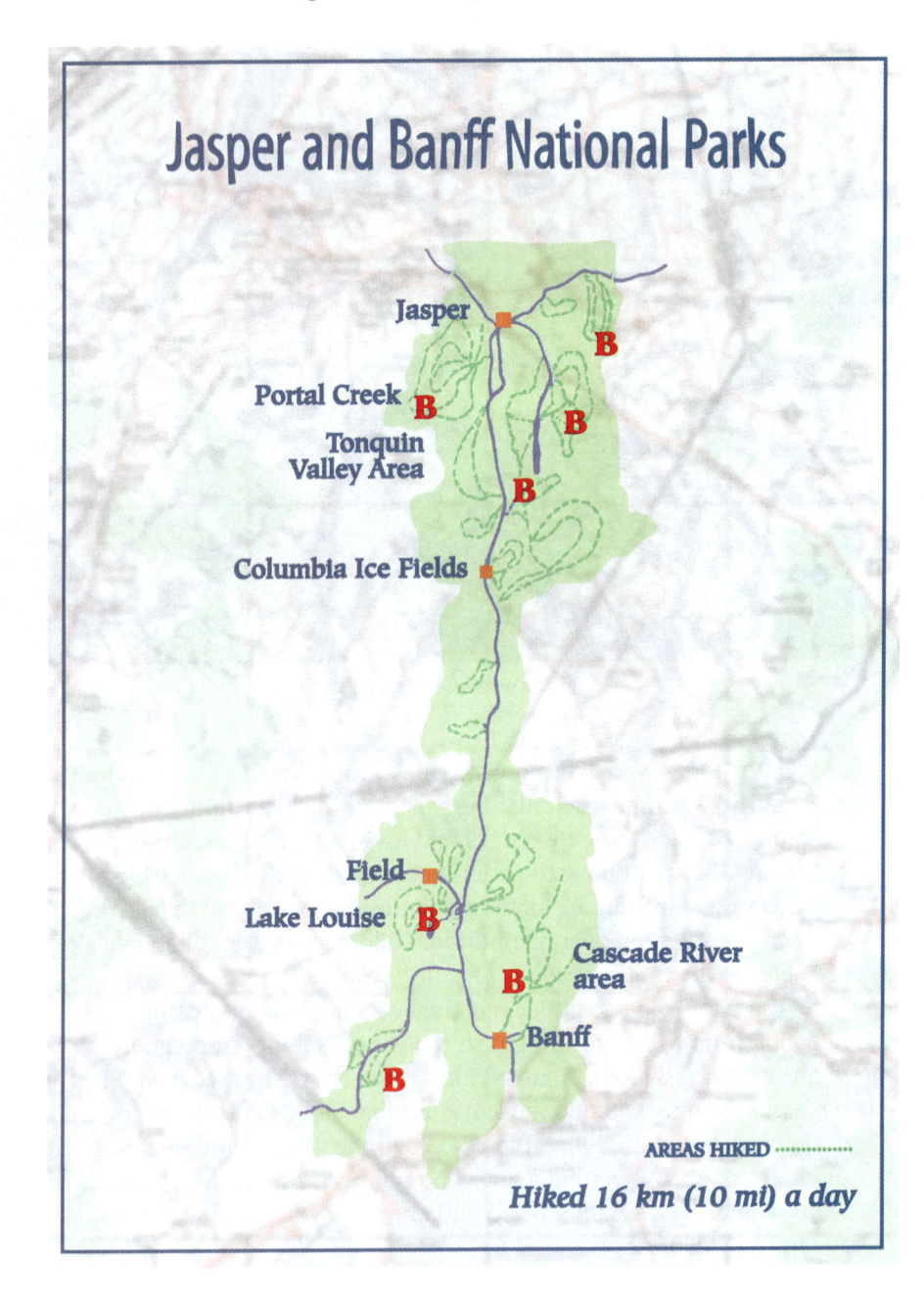

Jasper and Banff National Parks

- Jasper
- Portal Creek
- Tonquin Valley Area
- Columbia Ice Fields
- Field
- Lake Louise
- Cascade River area
- Banff

AREAS HIKED ....

Hiked 16 km (10 mi) a day

4

Jasper National Park

Portal Creek is a small stream that originates high in the mountains and flows downward until it reaches the Athabasca River. Along this stream is a hiking trail popular with both hikers and horseback riders. Past the Portal Creek camping area, about four kilometres up the trail, awaits some spectacular scenery—rock slides, snow-capped mountains, and alpine meadows. But the best is yet to come; another four kilometres along the trail is a second campground, located at the beginning of the Tonquin Valley.

If you imagine yourself on a large hill overlooking a sculpted green valley and a winding blue stream, surrounded by mountains, you will have pictured what it is like in the Tonquin Valley. On both sides of the trail leading to the valley are thousands of sub-alpine flowers such as the Indian paintbrush, elephant head flowers, black-eyed Susans, columbines, fireweed, violets, thistles, and many others. The green meadows are blanketed with cotton grass, moss campions, white and pink mountain heather, and other flowers. Ground squirrels scurry among the rocks, and there are hoary marmots, pikas, weasels, ptarmigans, and various types of insects. The meadows attract caribou, grizzly bears, foxes, coyotes, wolverines, hawks, and owls.

Above the meadows loom the snowcapped mountains adding to the majestic beauty of the area. However, the reality of the experience, as always, far exceeds any description. Thus I would urge anyone who values the wonders of nature to explore this remarkable valley.

Beyond the Tonquin Valley campground lies one of the most popular fishing spots in Jasper National Park—Amethyst Lake. The water is frigid, but the lake is a fisherman's paradise, surrounded by incredible beauty; there are tall mountains and several small glaciers. This is a wonderful place.

I should mention that the Portal Creek area has an unfortunate connection with encounters between bears and humans. Near the Tonquin campground is a grave that marks the site where a park warden was killed by a grizzly many years ago. More recently, the area attracted national attention after a grizzly attack on two tourists in September 1992. I will discuss this incident in detail later in the chapter, but I want to assure anyone interested in visiting Portal Creek that the occurrence was extremely unusual. Indeed, it need not have happened at all, and should in no way discourage anyone from experiencing what the area has to offer. I have travelled the Portal Creek trail more than any other in North America and highly recommend it.

On one of my first visits to this area, I hiked for about two hours until I reached the Portal Creek camping area. I set up my tent and had a quick lunch, then travelled on to the alpine zone, about an hour's journey beyond the first campground. McCarrib Pass, as always, was breathtaking, and I stood there gazing at its rugged beauty for a few moments, before beginning the gradual climb to the highest point on the pass.

My plan was to find a good vantage point for observing any movement in the valley below; I certainly had a good view, but all I could see, far below, were the grey and yellow shapes of Columbian ground squirrels, scurrying from burrow to burrow, their loud chirps filling the air.

Portal Creek.

This chirping serves as a warning to other ground squirrels that there is danger in the area. My presence, in this case, was what had set them off, but usually their calls signal the approach of more dangerous intruders, such as grizzlies.

I had hoped to see some bears that I could photograph, but I realized I would have to look elsewhere, so I decided to hike to the other side of the pass. As I set out, I noticed a marmot standing on its hind legs,

Tonquin Valley and Amethyst Lake.

whistling. Marmots look like oversized groundhogs—as heavy as fourteen kilograms—and they can be grey, black, or white. They make their homes in burrows they dig beneath large rocks. The marmot's whistle is very similar to that of a human being, and the sound can tell a hiker a great deal about activity in the area; most importantly, from my point of view, the whistle has a lot to do with the activity of bears.

If a grizzly approaches an area and hears a marmot's whistling, the bear will attempt to hone in on the source of the music. If the bear is able to narrow it down to a certain burrow, then that marmot will never sing again. Similarly, if a bear hears a person whistling, it will attack what appears to be a giant whistling marmot. That is why I always talk to encourage a bear to move away—whistling would have the opposite effect.

Marmots often display very strange behaviour, and today they were acting oddly indeed—not so much the first one, but two others, a few metres away. They were standing on their hind legs, face to face, eyeball to eyeball. A moment later, these odd marmots took to furiously slapping one another, then got their paws around each other's throats and tried to choke each other. This bizarre spectacle continued for a few more minutes, at which point the marmots glared at one another and went back to eating grass. I never did figure out the cause of the commotion, so after a good laugh I continued on.

    I had walked about a kilometre from the nutty marmots when I noticed that everything was suddenly quite still. The single whistle of a marmot broke the silence, then all was quiet again. Looking around nervously, I realized that the cause of this strange lull was an approaching grizzly, light in colour, moving in a crisscross pattern towards me. The bear was about a hundred metres away and coming closer.

    The silence was quickly replaced by a chorus of chirping and squeaking, as nervous marmots and squirrels darted for the cover of their burrows. Meanwhile, the bear moved along the hillside, sniffing at each animal's burrow as he passed it by. One squirrel stuck its head out of its hole and squeaked just as the grizzly moved in the direction of its underground hiding place. The bear raced over to the burrow and began digging wildly; the trapped rodent surely would have been a late afternoon snack had a nearby marmot's whistle not proved enough of a distraction for the squirrel to make its escape. Thwarted, the bear stopped digging and raced across the hillside, but luckily for the squirrels, marmots, and me, it did not return.

Two marmots at each other's throats.

    Darkness was beginning to fall, so I began to hike back to the Portal Creek campground. As I was leaving the alpine zone, I spotted a beautiful adult silver-tipped grizzly boar browsing in the grass. He began to dig for roots in much the same way that he would hunt for ground squirrels and marmots—but without the intensity of the search for a live quarry. A grizzly reaches forward with its front paw to dig, pushing its claws into the ground, then shifting its body to pull away the topsoil. This process easily exposes the roots, which the bear gathers in its claws and eats, on the spot. The Portal Creek area is littered with holes that have been dug by bears searching for roots or burrowing animals.

I continued watching the silver-tipped grizzly tear at the vegetation; he may have known I was watching, but he ignored my presence. Casually, he turned his back on me and slowly wandered up an adjacent hill, occasionally digging for more roots. Near the bear, a pine marten slithered its way among the rocks where it captured and devoured a golden-mantled squirrel. All the time I was snapping photographs; there is no lack of subject matter in nature.

I continued to hike in the area for the next twenty-six days, starting out each day from the trailhead, journeying to McCarrib Pass and then returning to my campsite. The round trip was about twenty kilometres—an excellent way to get in good physical shape.

At the tail end of my twenty-six hikes, I finally got lucky, arriving at the meadow just as a sow and her cub were leaving the alpine zone after digging for squirrels. I took a great number of photographs and shot some film footage as well, thankful that my patience had finally paid off. I was feeling much better about my whole trip, even though I was accompanied on my return trip by what I can only describe as a tropical downpour. I have often wondered if there is a rain cloud that stays in this area waiting for me to arrive. Whatever the explanation, hiking in this area requires determination and patience—and a great raincoat. But I wasn't going to get depressed about the weather. I had gotten at least a few good pictures, and after a month of hiking, my legs were as hard as rocks and I felt terrific.

A few weeks later, I returned to Portal Creek for even more punishment. It was sunny the day I arrived; maybe I would escape the wrath of the hovering rain cloud. I was just approaching McCarrib Pass when I noticed a grizzly cub. Realizing that its mother could well be close by, I moved behind a cluster of bushes to get out of sight—but I was too late. The grizzly sow suddenly appeared right next to me and immediately began to close the three-metre gap that separated us. For a moment I panicked and could not remember what to do; but this was no time to lose control, and my rationality quickly returned. I dropped to the ground and covered my head with my hands.

The grizzly approached my prostrate body and systematically sniffed me from head to toe, her sniffs punctuated with occasional grunts. Although my heart was pounding and my adrenaline racing, I managed to find my voice. "I love you," I whispered. "Please don't eat me." Miraculously, the grunting became more and more faint—she was wandering away. After a long moment, I looked up and was relieved to see that the grizzlies were continuing on towards the meadow at a casual pace.

The encounter did not seem to affect either of the bears at all; they began to graze calmly in the meadow. I, on the other hand, was shaking, and my heart continued to pound for some time; the incident had certainly given me a start—and almost an ending. Luckily, I was not hurt, but I was not about to leave the area entirely unscathed. It was raining again. I shook my fist at the sky and hiked out.

I returned to Portal Creek area for another visit the following summer. After two unsuccessful hikes, I began a third trip in, and as I neared the high point of McCarrib Pass, I noticed a young grizzly about thirty metres away. This bear was frantically digging for a squirrel; dirt flew in all directions as he got closer to his prey, and the frenzy lasted for about six minutes before he finally sat back on his rump to enjoy his meal. After supper, the grizzly wandered up a hill, sniffing several more holes as he passed, and occasionally stopping to munch the grass.

Sow grizzly charging.

The next morning, I crawled out of my tent before the sun had peeked out from behind the mountains. This is always a spectacular and beautiful time of the day. I returned to the meadow, hoping to see the same bear as the day before; the lower part of the meadow was empty, but on the hillside to my right was a sow digging for a squirrel. It was not the same bear, but I was not disappointed in my efforts to get some more mother-and-child photos—a bear cub was standing beside the sow. The cub was on the lookout for anything unusual, and very alert, because he immediately caught sight of my movements. As I stopped fiddling with my camera, the cub stared at me, apparently uncertain what to do.

Silver-tipped grizzly.

A few moments later, the sow grizzly poked her head out of the hole and looked my way. Much to my dismay, she left the cub's side and started moving towards me. I began taking pictures, hopeful that the approaching bear would turn back, but she continued advancing, and about ten metres away from me, started to circle my position. I remained calm and continued running my movie camera before realizing that I was inadvertently annoying her because of the sound my camera was making. The last thing I wanted to do at that point was to get on her bad side, so I stopped the camera, and that seemed to work. The sow turned and went back to the cub, and the two of them walked up a hillside and left the area. It was beginning to rain—of course!—so I headed out.

Late that night I heard grunting; and, as I always do in these situations, began my usual talk, explaining to the furry intruder how much I love all animals and thus deserve to be spared. The sounds quickly stopped. Maybe it was not my voice that scared bears away, as I had always thought—or even my topics of conversation. It occurred to me that there may be another explanation for the hasty departure, at least of last night's visitor. I had my sneakers in the tent, and as anyone who has hiked through mud in sneakers will attest, the smell is terrible. The repulsive smell in the tent that night is probably the reason that the bear decided not to stick around. I am seriously considering selling my used sneakers as a bear repellent; I could probably make a fortune.

Talking to bears has always been my practice, but on longer trips, I have noticed myself talking to all the animals and even to the flowers. When I get to this point, I realize I have been in the woods too long and it is time to leave. Once, when I actually caught myself saying goodbye to the flowers, I knew it was time for me to re-connect with the human race. I was near Portal Creek so I decided to follow it to where it emptied into the Athabasca River. I encountered a young black bear along the way; he was feeding on soopalie berries and did not seem to mind my presence. Soon after, a larger bear wandered out of the forest into the area, and the two of them were close enough to each other to frame in my camera. I got a few shots before the bigger bear spotted his neighbour and began to chase him into the woods. I heard some scratching noises coming from a nearby thicket, so I moved closer in the hopes of getting some more pictures.

The small bear had climbed a tree, and the larger one was sitting at the bottom, looking up, obviously amused. It was quite a comical moment. I figured the bears were becoming as crazy as I was, so I left the area. After weathering the usual downpour I arrived safely at my car and returned to civilization.

******

Over the years, I have shown my bear safety program several times at the Jasper Park Lodge and the Jasper Legion. I have always believed that sharing my experiences and images of the outdoors at various venues in Jasper is an excellent way of educating tourists who visit the area: they learn a lot about the local wildlife and, more importantly, they find out how to avoid getting into difficulties with bears.

In the summer of 1992, I was putting my program on at the Jasper legion hall and had made arrangements to do the same at the Jasper museum for the rest of the summer.

When I arrived at the Jasper information centre, I inquired about the possibility of camping at Portal Creek for about a month, as I had done in the past. I knew that spending a month in the area would result in me getting some more great pictures for my upcoming nature program. The attendant told me that I was only allowed to spend three nights in a row at any campground, which is understandable, since so many hikers now use the facilities, unlike years ago when they were virtually empty and you could stay at a given site as long as you wanted to. But she added that I was not allowed to take pictures for my intended purpose in the park, which surprised and disappointed me. Needless to say, I protested, and eventually I was referred to a park official who confirmed that I could only camp in each area for a limited time and, on learning that I was showing a bear safety program at the museum and that I was preparing a slide show for the schools I would be visiting the following year, advised me I needed a business licence for this kind of activity. I got the impression that this bureaucrat intended to block my museum program, but I tried to be pleasant and asked where I could obtain the licence.

Black bear sitting.

Obviously displeased with my forced calmness, he asked me to leave the park. I was shocked, but it did occur to me that his hostility might stem from the fear that I would raise park safety issues in my presentations that could reflect badly on park officials. Now I knew I would be hassled by the staff. But, I intended to describe our exchange to the students I would be visiting during the school year, and I told him so.

Jasper is truly a magnificent park, but some of the people who run the park are far from magnificent. Still, I persevered in my effort to show my program by trying to obtain the necessary licence from the city manager. He told me matter-of-factly that he would only consider allowing my programs to proceed after discussing the matter with the park wardens. The problem was, the program was scheduled to begin at the Jasper museum that evening, and I knew I could never obtain approval in time—if ever. My program had been widely promoted, and I knew people would be disappointed if I cancelled. I myself was extremely disappointed but decided to cancel the talks for the rest of the summer. I just didn't want to be subjected to official harrassment.

Despite the difficulty I was having with park officials, I decided not to let it ruin an otherwise excellent summer. I once again hiked up the Portal Creek trail with the hope of seeing some bears in the alpine zone and taking more pictures. The weather was great for the moment, and although I saw no bears, I did manage to photograph ground squirrels, a marmot, and two hawks. After I had hiked past Portal Creek campsite, a large, chocolate-coloured grizzly suddenly appeared at a turn in the trail. The bear was about ten metres away with his nose to the ground and, as I knew he had not yet seen me, I slowly backed up, then moved about nine metres off the trail; after about a minute or so, the bear passed by, and wandered out of sight into the bushes.

The next morning, I stopped at the information centre to advise the attendant that I had seen a bear heading towards the first campsite at Portal Creek. The attendant thanked me and hurriedly sent me on my way. This struck me as odd; if a bear is sighted on a trail or near a campsite, a full report is usually taken and most times the trail is immediately closed. I have reported bear sightings in parks throughout Alaska, British Columbia, and Alberta, and this was the first time I was not taken seriously. I was concerned but decided not to pursue it further.

Soon afterward, I left the Jasper area and went hiking in northern British Columbia and Alaska, returning at the end of August to find an article about me in the local paper, the *Jasper Booster*. The write-up discussed the cancelled bear programs and outlined the concerns I had about advice being given to tourists visiting the national park.

A highlight of the newspaper piece was my criticism of the vagueness and inaccuracy of a Parks Canada pamphlet, *You Are In Bear Country*—supposedly a set of guidelines to educate tourists about bears. I was particularly struck by the recommendation to whistle in the woods as a method of scaring bears away. This is not good advice as I have mentioned before. My experience, on the Portal Creek trail and elsewhere, is that whistling attracts bears; they associate the sound with one of their favourite meals—marmots. It is probably because my talks earlier in the summer included this kind of information, which conflicted with Parks Canada's prevailing wisdom, that the park official effectively forced me to cancel my remaining programs. I knew the article would not serve to improve the already strained relationship between me and the park officials; nevertheless, I was gratified that my concerns were being openly discussed.

To escape any further controversy, I headed up the Portal Creek trail yet again. Bear tracks and droppings were everywhere, so I knew my chances of seeing a bear were very good. After setting up my campsite for the night, I hiked towards the high meadows, but there were no bears around and it was getting dark, so I returned to my tent. To my surprise, my "personal" rain cloud was nowhere to be seen!

After a restful night and a hearty breakfast, I took down my tent and returned to the alpine meadows, which were buzzing with activity. Several ground squirrels were feeding on grass and flowers, occasionally pausing to chase each other playfully. Then, the shadow of a hawk stopped the fun; the squirrels darted for cover, quickly scurrying into their burrows. Farther along the valley, I saw a weasel moving along the shoreline of a small stream. I assumed that this weasel was hunting for squirrels, but in this case, it was the weasel that was being pursued—by a large ground squirrel.

Weasels are said to be the most bloodthirsty animals alive and are savage hunters. The only explanation for this turn of events was that the squirrel was protecting her young. After capturing this unusual incident on film, I continued hiking. As I neared the second Portal Creek campground, the sun was just beginning to dip below the mountain tops. Wonder of wonders, there was *still* no rain.

Just as it became too dark to take pictures, a lost photo opportunity presented itself. Three bears—a grizzly sow and two yearlings—emerged from the shrubs and wandered up the hillside. I watched this bear family until they faded out of sight, then pitched my tent and settled in for the night. There are few pleasures in life that are more rewarding than relaxing beside a cosy campfire, and the clear, moonlit sky made the experience even more peaceful.

Early the next morning I hiked to Moat Lake, a relatively short journey that can take two hours or more because the trail, a popular route for horseback riders, is extremely muddy. For those prepared to take on the ardours of this hike, the beauty of the area is more than adequate compensation. That day, there was icing on the cake—a rainbow.

I noticed several grizzly tracks in the shallow part of the lake, which indicated that a bear had been there recently, searching for the discarded portions of a previously caught fish. This bear must have been hungry, because its tracks extended forty-five metres into the frigid water; unfortunately, it was no longer around for me to photograph. Disappointed, I returned to McCarrib Pass.

Just as I reached Portal Creek campground, I spotted a large, chocolate-coloured grizzly wandering through the grounds, about fifteen metres from the tenting area. It was the same bear I had seen in the area a month earlier. The grizzly, head to the ground, sniffed his way over to the stream and stuck his nose in the water—in the spot where, a few days earlier, I had seen a hiker cleaning his dishes. Then he headed out of sight in the direction of the food poles provided by the park for hanging food out of the reach of animals.

I believed there was a good chance that the grizzly would return that night, so I left the area and went back to where my car was parked. After all the trips I had taken along the Portal Creek trail, I knew it extremely well, and decided that it would be safe to hike out, even though it was dark. Just the same, I talked and sang loudly all the way to discourage any bears that might be prowling around.

A weasel.

It was well after midnight when I got to the car. Early the next morning at the information centre I told the same park attendant to whom I had reported my previous bear sighting about my second sighting of the chocolate-coloured grizzly. With a curt "Thank you," she turned away—just as she had done the previous time. Considering all the trouble I was having with Parks Canada officials that summer, I was not surprised at her attitude; they had probably warned their staff to avoid me.

By this time I was disgusted with Parks Canada, and decided to visit one of my other favourite bear spots at Fish Creek, in Alaska, near the community of Hyder. In that area, my credentials had never been questioned. Just before showing my bear program at the elementary school in nearby Stewart, British Columbia, one of the teachers inquired if I had heard about the man killed by a bear in Jasper National Park. She was not sure if the tragedy had occurred on the Portal Creek trail. Although I gave a few more talks and presentations at nearby schools, I was distracted and upset by the news of the killing, so I made plans to return to the Jasper area.

Back in Alberta, I immediately went for a hike up the Portal Creek trail, towards the alpine meadows of the Tonquin Valley. Although the weather was fine, the trail was very muddy; could some rain actually have fallen in my absence? It was hard to believe, but then it had also been unusually dry in the period before my departure for Alaska; apparently, the gods of precipitation had decided to favour me. But I was about to experience another of nature's surprises. As soon as I began to climb to higher elevations, it began to snow. Some higher areas are snowbound all year; nevertheless, there was quite a bit of the white stuff—fifteen centimetres—where I began climbing, which made hiking difficult.

One of the advantages of hiking in the snow is that bear tracks are much easier to find, and it was not long before I spotted a fresh set of paw prints. I followed them and after half an hour, I came upon the bear in a pleasant meadow. The tracks indicated that the bear had gone in a circle; it was now making its way towards the Portal Creek campground where I had stayed before going to Alaska.

This encounter prompted me to go back to town to find out all I could about the unfortunate incident I had learned about in Hyder. It was as I had suspected: the tragedy had indeed taken place at the Portal Creek campground; an European tourist had died. Details were sketchy, but I knew a report of the incident would be in the local paper. Before checking into it further, I went to the Parks Canada information booth in Jasper and told the attendant about the bear I had seen the previous day. This time, instead of being ignored, she questioned me for more than ten minutes about the sighting.

The attendant was particularly interested in the direction the bear was headed, and double-checked my statement several times. This new attitude was encouraging, but I was furious that officials had not shown such concern earlier. If they had, the death might have been avoided; only sixteen days before the bear attack, I had warned the attendant that a bear

Rainbow near Moat Lake.

was in the Portal Creek area; she had not responded to my warning. Now a man was dead and a woman had been seriously injured. I also wondered what might have happened if I had been allowed to show my bear program through the summer months; perhaps the two hikers could have obtained the information they needed to avoid the tragedy.

I soon learned the details of the accident, which had occurred on September 15. It had been a cold week in the Portal Creek area, and several centimetres of snow had fallen at McCarrib Pass, leaving the trail muddy and the campground covered with snow. Despite the treacherous conditions, two tourists decided to go hiking in the area.

The two English hikers, Cherry Reksten and Trevor Percy Lancaster, arrived at the campground late in the afternoon carrying heavy knapsacks. They put their packs on a picnic table and wandered off to explore the campsite.

On returning to retrieve her pack from the picnic table, Cherry spied a grizzly coming straight toward her. Turning her back, she quickly walked to a clump of bushes nearby. The bear continued toward her. There was a tree among the bushes, which Cherry climbed. Trevor, who was close by when the bear appeared, also began searching for a place of safety.

Undoubtedly, they were both terrified. It is difficult to think clearly in such a situation; often a person reacts instinctively or panics. But thus far, the two hikers had reacted well.

Unfortunately, the grizzly continued to pursue Cherry. He lumbered over to the tree, stood on his hind legs, and grabbed at one of Cherry's boots as she climbed, pulling it off. Cherry, understandably, began to scream for help.

Trevor, who was not far away, heard her frantic screams and shouted to her to climb down from the tree and run. Cherry took his advice and was able to avoid the bear for a moment, but he gave chase and quickly knocked her down. He tore at the back of Cherry's head, bit her on the neck, and began to claw at her back. Trevor ran to her defence, attempting to distract the bear.

The grizzly immediately turned on Trevor and began to maul him. Even in his plight, Trevor was more concerned about Cherry's condition than his own safety. "Just run for it!" he urged her. "Run for it, Cherry—it's O.K." Bleeding and panic-stricken, Cherry made it to a tent about a hundred metres away.

In the tent, another backpacker, Jim Murakami, quickly responded to Cherry's pleas for help: he scrambled outside and assisted the injured woman to a nearby rock slide, where he believed they would be safe. Then they made their way onto the Portal Creek trail.

Jim told Cherry to wait on the trail while he ran for help, but she decided to keep walking, convinced the bear would come after her. At a crest on the trail, she looked back towards the campground only to see her companion still being mauled by the grizzly; the terrible sight plunged her deeper into shock, but she forced herself to keep walking.

It was not until seven o'clock that evening that a helicopter carrying wardens and paramedics arrived at the campground and landed about two hundred metres away from the tenting area. The wardens spotted the bear when it reared its head above some willow bushes where it had taken cover. Trevor's body, already partly eaten, lay nearby. The grizzly was shot and killed.

Cherry was found about six kilometres away from where the attack had occurred; she was rushed to Seton General Hospital in Jasper, then transferred to the University of Alberta Hospital in Edmonton, where she underwent extensive plastic surgery on her scalp.

It is my belief that the Portal Creek campground needs a number of improvements so that any future accidents can be avoided. A number of times when I have stayed there, I have seen campers cleaning fish and cooking utensils in the creek that runs directly in front of the campground. This attracts a large number of small animals—porcupines, squirrels, pikas, and mice—that scavenge in the area, looking for crumbs or fish parts. If these small animals are finding food, it stands to reason that larger animals, such as bears, also forage in the area. Park officials should put up a sign warning campers not to keep food anywhere near their tents and urging them to wash dishes and clean fish at a safe distance from the campground.

Grizzly at McCarrib Pass.

Another concern I have is that the campground is not set up in the triangle method—that is, the eating area, food storage site, and tenting spot are kept at least ninety metres apart. At the moment, campers cook, eat, and sleep in the same area; this poor arrangement will surely lead to further trouble. As well, the bear pole is much too close to the campground. Properly, it should be at least ninety metres from the tenting and eating areas; the pole is now only thirty-eight metres from the picnic tables, and the tables are twenty-three metres from the first tent site.

Until these concerns are addressed, the Portal Creek campground will not be safe.

As to the hikers' actions in trying to escape the grizzly, these too could have been influenced by better and more complete information from Parks Canada. They could have been advised to slowly back away when they first spotted the bear, or to adopt the fetal position when attacked, which is exactly what I would have advised if I had been permitted to present my program that summer. I am not saying they would definitely have been able to prevent what happened, but they would at least have had a chance—and perhaps it would not have proved necessary to kill the bear.

Since the attack took place, I have been interviewed by Cherry Reksten's legal counsel, and I have told them the events of the previous summer regarding my sightings at Portal Creek and my dealings with park officials. During one meeting with the lawyers, I was given copies of several documents prepared by the warden's office in Jasper, which showed that during the relevant period, the only recorded sighting in the Portal Creek area was of a mother bear and two cubs. In other words, there was no record of the bear sightings I had reported to them, on July 6 and August 30. Just as I had feared, the park attendant I told about the chocolate-coloured grizzly did not take the information I gave her seriously; in fact she made no report either time.

I still get upset when I think of this. All the other parks I have visited have been staffed by people who take my safety concerns seriously, and their standard procedure is to close a trail if a bear is spotted on it, or is close to a campground. I wish the Jasper park officials had spent as much time paying attention to the bear reports as they did trying to run me out of the park. Park wardens should ensure that all bear sightings are immediately recorded and passed along the chain of command—whether or not officials happen to be having a difference of opinion with one of the people providing them with information. Under no circumstances should any report be taken lightly. As a matter of interest, I asked for a federal inquiry. I learned later that the park official who had asked me to leave the park was removed from his position there during the summer of 1994 and relocated. Now all the park officials in Jasper are very conscious of bear safety.

The Portal Creek area is magnificent, and I hope precautions will be taken to ensure this area is not the sight of another bear attack. Although I still love Portal Creek and the Tonquin Valley, it is difficult not to think of the bear attack when I am in the area. The last time I hiked on the trail, it poured rain as never before—but I hardly noticed.

5

The Spatsizi Plateau

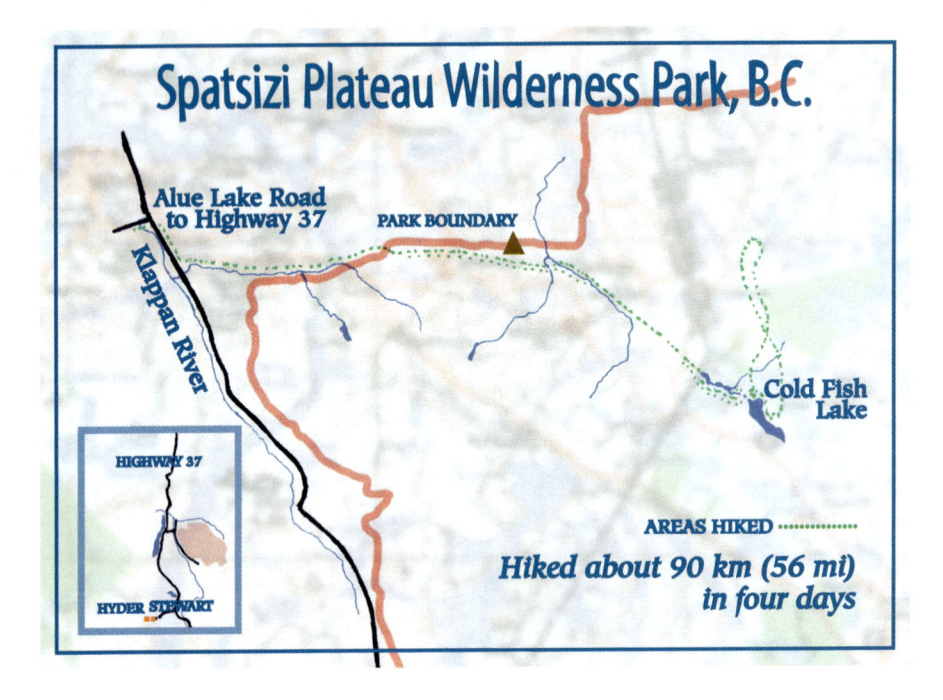

Spatsizi Plateau Wilderness Park, B.C.

Alue Lake Road to Highway 37
PARK BOUNDARY
Klappan River
Cold Fish Lake
HIGHWAY 37
HYDER STEWART
AREAS HIKED
Hiked about 90 km (56 mi) in four days

Jim
Kahl, a good friend of mine from Toutle, Washington, is an extremely enthusiastic nature-lover who has accompanied me on a number of outdoor adventures. Apart from teaching outdoor education at Washington State College, he is an avid farmer and spends his spare time kayaking, mountain climbing, or hiking. The only thing that I have never been able to figure out about Jim is why he enjoys hiking with me; our approach to hiking is as different as night and day. Jim is organized and efficient, and always has the latest in camping gear, while my equipment is often quite dilapidated and my methods tend to be scattered. Like me, Jim has noted these differences—and pointed out that I am unlike not only him, but the rest of humanity as well. This comment was in reference to the "provisions" I took along for myself on a four-day hike: one sandwich. No tent, no sleeping bag. Just the sandwich. Jim also expressed a certain amount of surprise that I had survived the trip.

Each summer, Jim and I try to go on at least one hiking trip somewhere in western Canada or Alaska. In the summer of 1992, we decided to hike to the Spatsizi Plateau, in northern British Columbia. It was dark when we arrived, so we set up our tents about two kilometres from the trailhead. Jim is one of the few people I know who is as excited as I am about hiking in new areas and looking for bears, but on this trip he was feeling nervous because he had a nosebleed—and blood can attract bears. But his desire to observe and photograph bears overcame any anxiety, and we agreed to try to keep a safe distance between ourselves and our furry friends. The next morning, we were raring to go. The hike we had planned is fifty kilometres—one way—but Jim and I are both in good shape, so the distance was no deterrent. Jim is a very determined hiker; once he begins hiking, he does not quit until he reaches his destination.

We woke at dawn, packed our gear and began the long hike towards the plateau. The weather had been bad, and quite a few trees had been blown across the path, forcing us to slow our pace considerably in order to negotiate the obstacle course they had created. I wondered whether my old nemesis, the Portal Creek storm cloud, was responsible.

But if we thought the fallen trees were reason to complain, we were in for a real challenge in the form of what appeared to be the world's largest marsh—an Atlantic Ocean among bogs—and we had expected to just walk right through it. Jim was as determined as ever, so we made our way along this "trail" for several kilometres, sometimes hiking in water up to our knees. It came as no surprise that we fell short of our intended goal for that day, setting up camp after "only" thirty kilometres.

As we pitched the tent (Jim's, of course!), I noticed some blood trickling from Jim's nose, but neither of us was very worried. The hike had been harder than we anticipated, and all we were thinking about was food and a good night's sleep. We were just sitting down to eat when I noticed some bushes moving behind Jim. Not wanting to startle him with this news, I surreptitiously kept an eye on the bushes for any further movement and, as we continued our meal, I kept one hand on a large frying pan—just in case. After supper, we hung our backpacks (with the food inside) on trees that were about ninety metres from the tent; my pack was about three metres above the ground, while Jim's was a couple of metres higher. When Jim saw my pack, he shook his head worriedly. "It's not high enough," he said. Imagine, questioning the expertise of the bear man! I smiled and assured him that my pack was just fine.

Jim did not seem satisfied with my response, but he was too tired to argue. We crawled into our sleeping bags and were just dozing off when we heard a loud crash. Jim jumped up and stuck his head out of the tent. "My gosh, it's a bear and he has your food," he whispered angrily. "I told you that backpack was not high enough." Well, even so-called experts can be wrong.

We tried to remain calm, but within a few moments, we just had to look outside again. We could hear the grizzly grappling with my backpack. Luckily, the interloper was not near the tree that held Jim's pack, and this was good news; some of our provisions might survive.

As we watched, the bushes to our right shook. From the sounds of it, the thief was dragging my pack away. Because the bear was apparently leaving, Jim suggested checking to see whether his knapsack was safe. He leapt out of the tent, handed me a can of bear spray, and ordered, "Cover me." Then, Jim rushed over to "his" tree—to his delight, his pack was untouched.

Jim immediately strung a rope between two trees and suspended the backpack well out of reach of the bear; meanwhile, I stood watch with the can of spray. We could still hear the bear crashing through the bushes, but the sound was growing fainter and we estimated that he was about forty meters away. The bushes were moving in the distance, but we could no longer see the bear.

Shaken by the incident, Jim and I cautiously returned to the tent and tried to relax. But Jim, unnerved by what had happened, began wondering whether the bear might come back for seconds. "What should we do?" he demanded. "Don't worry," I said. "The bear got my food, so he's not interested in us." Jim sensed the uncertainty in my voice; he was right. We decided to take turns sleeping; I volunteered to take the first watch, and immediately fell asleep—but not for long.

I came awake with a start as Jim shook me, exclaiming, "Wake up! Wake up! How can you sleep with a grizzly roaming around our tent?"

"Jim, don't worry," I answered. "If the bear had wanted to eat us, he would have done it by now." In retrospect, I don't think this was the reassurance Jim was looking for. In fact, he got more and more agitated,

Spatsizi Plateau.

and finally I found out the real reason.

"I have *got* to go to the bathroom. What am I going to do?" Evidently, Jim was afraid the bear would get him while he was relieving himself. I sympathized; if you were going to die, that wouldn't be a very glamorous exit.

"Go outside and go to the bathroom," I told Jim. "The bear won't bother you."

I'm not sure if Jim believed me, but he did leave the tent, and came back a few minutes later, unharmed. We laughed about our predicament then tried to get some sleep.

Throughout the night, we heard the bear moving around in the bushes, but the sounds were not all that close by. Still, we were fairly nervous—that's probably why we could make out even those faint noises—and we spent a restless night. The next morning, Jim was very quiet as we got up early to pack our gear and continue along the trail. We

The Cold Fish Lake area.

still had the food Jim had brought, so we would be all right, and I assured Jim that I would catch some trout to make up for what the bear had taken. As we started hiking, we both kept an eye out for the bear and my missing backpack but saw neither. I was not about to make the possibly fatal mistake of searching for the pack—now the property of that grizzly—and although he said nothing, I was sure Jim was in agreement.

Jim set an extremely fast pace (possibly because there was a bear behind us, or so we thought), and after a few kilometres of his speed-walking, I found that trying to keep up was an impossible task. Besides, my left leg was sore and I began to limp. With Jim's encouragement, I was able to continue, but the trail was in miserable condition, and I began to wonder if anything would go right on this trip.

Jim and I must have been quite a sight as we staggered into the Cold Fish Lake campground; I was hobbling, he was still dealing with a bloody nose, and the two of us had been hiking for sixteen hours across swamps, over trees, and through mosquitoes the size of pumpkins. But we had made it, and our luck was about to change; we were informed by the camp caretaker that we could rent one of the cabins for six dollars each—a wood stove, firewood, two beds, and best of all, a roof. Jim and I had hiked to paradise.

After some much-needed rest, we spent the next day hiking near the lake. Jim discovered moose and grizzly tracks in several spots; they had been left recently, and this gave us hope that we might get some good pictures. That afternoon, I did some fishing, as I had promised Jim, and caught four large trout.

The following day, completely recovered from our ordeal, we decided to hike to the plateau, four kilometres away. On the way, we stopped frequently to take pictures of the spectacular scenery. The hike was particularly rewarding, and a light rain only added to the beauty that surrounded us. Raindrops illuminated many of the flowers and spider webs, and they glistened as the sun returned. I was glad we were there, despite the earlier mishaps.

Yellow Columbine.

Once again, I had to continually urge Jim to slow down because there was no way I could keep up with him. However, Jim had heard this excuse for slowing down on several of our previous trips, so he ignored my plodding pace and continued to hike at his own rate. I decided not to even bother telling him about my difficulties. I had discovered an incredible array of flowers that would be ideal for my slide program—at least, that's the story I would tell Jim.

This was not a complete rationalization because the array of flowers was spectacular, and it was difficult to pass them by without at least a glance. I must have given them quite the glance, though, because I was only halfway to the plateau when Jim got there. By the time I arrived, he looked fit to be tied! Perhaps he was totally disgusted with me. But we soon became absorbed in our surroundings: the view from the plateau was breathtaking, we could see for several kilometres in every direction. The plateau itself was unusual since instead of trees, there were enormous green meadows, dotted with large rocks and patches of ice and snow. As well, the flowers on the plateau were in full bloom.

Marmots whistled occasionally, and several ptarmigans scurried in front of us, but otherwise this was a very peaceful area. Jim and I had expected to see large animals on the plateau, but we were disappointed. Perhaps it was because the area has a hunting season that only small animals were in evidence. Nevertheless, the plateau was beautiful, and we continued to hike in this area until the sun was about to set then headed back to the camp. On our way down from the plateau, we spotted a moose on a hillside, but it was too far away to get any good photos. Well, at least we were able to see something bigger than a marmot, even if it was at a distance.

Jim Kahl.

Back at the camp, we struck up a friendly conversation with two other visitors who were also enjoying this spectacular area. They were just finishing their trip and were intending to leave the next day by float plane; after what we had been through, we decided to join them. But we were glad to have made the journey. Although it had not been the smoothest of trips, at least we had seen a bear—though not in ideal circumstances—and experienced some remarkable landscapes.

6

Spirit of the Rainforest

Most black bears are charcoal black, brown, or cinnamon-coloured, but in northern British Columbia lives a very unusual kind of black bear, which is actually white. Non-natives call this bear "Kermode," in reference to Francis Kermode, a curator of the British Columbia Museum in the early twentieth century. Another, more romantic name given to this rare animal is a Japanese term that translates as "dream bear."

Native cultures have achieved a special bond with nature, and they have a significant appreciation for these oddly coloured bears. In the Tsimshian language of the Indians of northern British Columbia, they are called *Moksgm'ol*, which means "white bear." Other native peoples refer to them as "ghost bears." The Natives regard the bear as a creature of great spiritual and cultural importance—a view I share—and many of the native people I have met consider bears part of the family and refer to them as brothers or sisters. According to Indian legend, a raven created bears, and he made every tenth bear white to remind us of the ice-age glaciers.

Black bear and spirit bear.

I heard several stories that white bears had been seen near Terrace, British Columbia. Uncertain whether these "spirit bears," as I called them, were myth or fact, I decided to find out the truth for myself. I began hiking in the Terrace area, on bear trails that led to and from the Skeena and Kitsumakalum rivers. The foliage in the area was extremely thick, and my movements created a continual rustling noise as I hiked. As a result, any nearby bears heard me coming, and were long gone by the time I arrived. After sixteen days, the best I could manage was the occasional glimpse of a wide pair of bear buttocks as its owner beat a hasty retreat—and this was not exactly an image worthy of the mythical creature I had come to find.

White bear with black bear cubs.

I knew that patience would be my best ally if I were going to properly study and photograph these white bears, so I continued to hike along the Kitsumakalum River, following a bear trail until I was able to find a large tree, suitable for a campsite and affording me an excellent view of two nearby meadows. I climbed the tree and set up camp about five metres above the ground, high enough to allow animals plenty of room to pass underneath. The shelter I built was made of some tree limbs, and I placed a piece of plastic overhead to act as a makeshift roof. I am always proud of my engineering feats, and this was one of my finest. Unfortunately, nature did not have the same respect for my building abilities, and after a four-hour downpour I was lying in a stream.

The next day, I caught sight of a black bear wandering through the meadow. The bear did not stay long, and he was not the colour I had hoped for, but at least the sighting did not consist of a retreating rump. My luck changed a few days later, however, when I spotted a mother bear and two cubs near my camp. The mother bear was creamy white, and the cubs were black with white patches on their chests. After many disappointing days and several wet nights, I had finally found what I had been seeking. The sow was definitely a spirit bear. She had probably mated with a pure black bear and created the two mixed cubs. It was exciting, but as quickly as they arrived they disappeared.

The following afternoon, my good luck continued. I spotted two more white bears. These bears had seen me before I had seen them, and they were both nervously standing on their hind legs. I stopped moving, and this had a calming effect on the bears. As I watched, they began to wrestle playfully; this made for some wonderful photographs. But a few moments later, both of them had vanished into the bushes.

I heard a bear underneath my camp that night, but the creaking, rickety structure must have made it nervous,

Two spirit bears.

and it quickly ran away. The next morning, not far away, I noticed a white bear travelling with a black bear through the woods. I was careful not to move, but the two bears immediately picked up my scent; the black bear reacted by quickly running away, while the startled white bear, a sow, ran over to a nearby tree and started climbing, until she reached two sturdy limbs. She rested there a while but never took her eyes off me. Knowing she was uncomfortable about my presence, I slowly backed away. As soon as I had done this, she climbed down the tree and bolted in the same direction the black bear had gone.

For the next few days, I had no luck spotting bears, but I did find myself engaged in battle with a squirrel. I was apparently intruding upon its tree, and each day the little creature would reproach me, chattering loudly and angrily. On the third day, the squirrel got so mad that it threw a pine cone at me, bouncing it off the top of my head. I would have gotten some sort of revenge, but a moose broke up our argument as she strolled by. I tried to stay motionless in my leafy perch, hoping not to scare the moose away; meanwhile, the squirrel was gathering more ammunition.

I looked down to see the moose's face right in front of me, so near that I could have touched her. Indeed, I was being treated to an extreme close-up of this moose. She was homely. On the other hand, she must have felt the same way about me—after giving me a quick once-over, she put her head down and quickly moved away. As an acorn bounced off my head, I began to wonder whether this meant I was at one with nature. Probably not.

For the next week, I continued to search the area, but I had no luck. By this time, the bears probably knew where I was hanging out, and they wanted nothing to do with a crazy person living in a tree. I decided to pack up my gear and try out a well-padded bear trail that I had seen nearby. In an extremely muddy spot along the trail, I noticed recent bear tracks and droppings. There was also a small stream, where

Moose staring at me.

the bears probably came to drink. I found a good lookout position and watched. As I surveyed the area, a small frog began hopping in a circle around me. That convinced me that my earlier musings on being in harmony with nature were wishful thinking.

I continued to watch the mud hole for several hours. Early in the afternoon, I finally saw a small black bear, which stayed for only a moment before heading back into the woods. For a moment, I thought the bear had caught my scent, but then I realized that he had sensed another bear. The approaching bear was not white, but rather a cream colour, and he looked to be about seventy-six kilograms in weight. He saw me immediately, but seemed unconcerned with my presence and continued walking towards the mud hole.

There, he waded out to the centre of a metre-deep puddle that I had not previously noticed, and lay down in the water. After a moment, he began rubbing his neck with his front paw and craning his neck in the air. Then he lowered his head into the water, placing his nose just beneath the surface. This bear must have been extremely warm to lie down in the middle of what was really no more than a hole.

Dream bear cooling off.

After cooling off, the bear left the water and began to eat grass, slowly lumbering out of sight as he ate. He hadn't done anything unusual, but I thought it was interesting to see a spirit bear take a bath. Native cultures have always believed that these bears have great power, and I was able to confirm this for myself. Just the sight of this bear, even going through its everyday activities, made me feel good.

7

Hanna and Tintina Creeks, British Columbia

The streams and rivers of northern British Columbia abound with fish, which assures a visitor of bear sightings. When I arrived at Hanna Creek, I was amazed at the numbers of sockeye salmon swimming in the stream—the water looked like a solid mass of fish.

Because my visit coincided with the salmon's spawning period, the male fish I saw had bright red bodies and light green heads, while the female salmon were dark red with green and yellow blotches. Among the multitudes of fish, I saw a few that easily weighed about four kilograms.

It was a beautiful time of year to be in this area; winter was coming soon, but for the moment everything was splendid. The mountain peaks were just beginning to change colour, from dark green to bright white, but the fresh snow on the mountainside was unable to overcome the heat of the afternoon sun, and small waterfalls were trickling down the steep mountain cliffs. Soon snow would cover this entire area.

The only distraction from all this splendour was a suffocating smell coming from the shore of Hanna Creek;

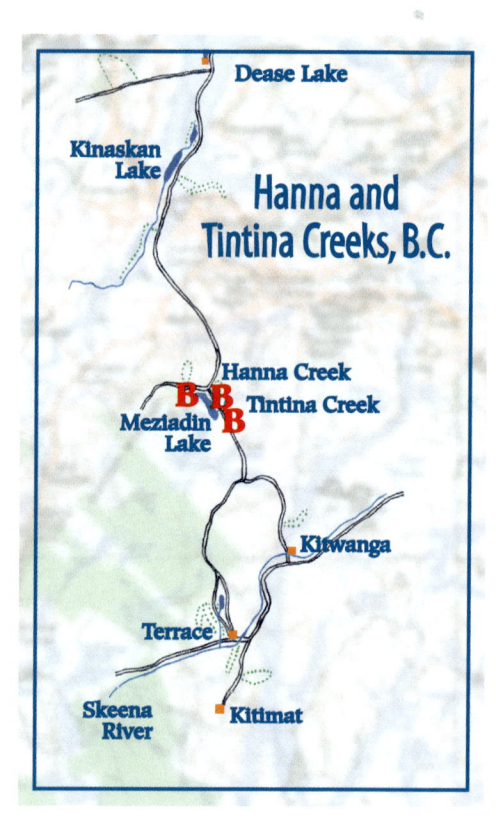

Hanna and Tintina Creeks, B.C.

a number of dead salmon were rotting along the shoreline. The odour had attracted several bald eagles, which intermittently fed on the carcasses. I watched the eagles eat their salmon dinner, and tried to take a few pictures. All was peaceful until a young grizzly darted out of the bushes about forty metres away, then started running towards me. I rose from my crouched position, slipped, and fell to the ground. Nothing seemed to be broken, so I sat upright and watched the bear.

He was still approaching—now within ten metres—but he had slowed from a run to a walk. Nevertheless, I began to mentally prepare my first line of defence—a speech explaining the importance of maintaining good relations between humans and animals. Just as I was about to begin, the bear came to a halt, as if he sensed that he was about to be subjected to something painfully boring. After staring at me for a moment, he turned and jumped into a bear tunnel. Considering I had just arrived at Hanna Creek, this was quite a welcome sight. My heart was still pounding, and I wondered whether such brief bear encounters might have long-term health effects.

With several years knocked off my life, I picked myself up and began walking downstream. Hanna Creek was very shallow, and there were several spots where the backs of the spawning salmon were halfway out of the stream. I continued walking, and every few moments I would glance behind me, just in case the young bear decided to declare war on me. When I arrived at the point where Hanna Creek flows into Meziadin Lake, I noticed that the fish were gathered in extremely large schools. Areas like these would make bears very happy.

I had the use of a canoe, which I thought would be a better way to see more of the area. I paddled from Meziadin Lake to Tintina Creek, a distance of 2.4 kilometres, and in this case an easy journey—the water was flowing slowly, and there was only a gentle current. After an hour of rowing, I arrived at a well-constructed beaver dam that was making life very difficult for many of the salmon that were trying to get through. They were trying to jump over the dam, but the distance was too great for several of them; the unfortunate ones became entangled in the wood and suffocated. The lifeless fish were brilliant red, and the colour made their twisted bodies beautiful even in death.

After portaging around the beaver dam, I returned to the water and continued paddling. I noticed wolf and grizzly tracks along the shoreline, so I steered towards deeper water. Ten minutes later I saw a cinnamon-coloured black bear about twenty metres ahead. He approached the stream and stopped right in front of me. I slowed the canoe down, but the bear did not seem to notice me. He was much too intent on the salmon. Suddenly, the bear began to frantically leap and pounce in the stream. The fish fled in every direction, and their red bodies streaked beneath my canoe.

For all his efforts, the cinnamon bear was not catching any fish, and this seemed to agitate him greatly. He ran downstream, stopped, then reversed his direction and headed towards me. Well, I was not to blame if this bear could not fish; I certainly would not blame *him* for *my* bad luck as a fisherman. So I stared at the approaching bear and said, "Hold it, hold it." The bear stopped and looked at me, then plunged his head into a shallow area and emerged with a salmon tightly clenched in his teeth. "You see," I called to him. "It wasn't my fault."

The cinnamon bear was excited at having caught a fish—a feeling I have only rarely experienced—and even deigned to give me a smile before returning to the bushes.

I was looking forward to more bear sightings, but soon afterward, a steady rain began to fall. I tried to hold out as long as I could, but several days passed, and it was still coming down. I surrendered and returned to civilization.

Cinnamon bear with sockeye salmon.

8

Kluane National Park, Yukon Territory

Kluane National Park, Yukon

- Destruction Bay
- Kluane Lake
- Sheep Mtn
- B
- B B
- Kaskawulsh Glacier
- Alaska Highway
- PARK BORDER
- Haines Junction
- Quill Creek
- Haines Road
- Kathleen Lake
- B

AREAS HIKED ············
Hiked approximately 9.7 km (6 mi) a day

The Yukon offers nature at its finest; there are many areas that remain untouched by the meddling hands of humanity, and few such places remain in the world. Visiting the Yukon is a true adventure because it is a wild, enchanting place.

A recent trip I took to the Yukon began on a sunny July day; the good weather presented an ideal opportunity to hike to the top of Sheep Mountain in Kluane National Park, just west of Kluane Lake and the Alaska Highway—a steep, challenging, six-kilometre route. At that time you could hike to Sheep Mountain directly from the highway. But because the hikers often disturbed the sheep grazing on the mountain, the park has designated a longer trail that takes you west to Sheep Bullion Plateau. The intermittent chirping and scurrying of Arctic ground squirrels distracted me from the monotonous trip, which took me three hours.

Sheep Mountain is well named, because just as I arrived at the top of the trail, I was greeted by about fifty dall sheep, which were grazing in the green meadows surrounded by rolling hills. Dall sheep are pure white, and since their habitat is covered with snow most of the year, the sheep are well camouflaged.

Most of the sheep in the meadows were ewes with their young; on a distant ridge, the rams were assembled in their own group. I noticed that two of them had broken horns, probably as the result of a mating season battle. Several others appeared to be quite old, because they had fully curled horns. In spring, grizzlies hunt dall sheep, usually focusing their attention on older animals such as those I saw, since they were probably easier targets. I took some pictures then returned to the hiker registration station near the base of the mountain.

The attendant at the station told me not to hike on one of the nearby trails—as many as eight grizzlies had been sighted in the area— then took me outside to show me the danger area, Sheep Bullion Plateau. This heightened my desire to see and photograph some bears, so I registered to hike the trail closest to the plateau, Kaskawulsh Glacier. Perhaps I would be lucky enough to observe bears there.

Beginning of Quill Creek.

As I headed towards the glacier trail, I passed the Sheep Bullion Plateau trail, and saw grizzly tracks and droppings everywhere. The temptation was so great that I decided to hike in the direction of the plateau. I felt guilty about ignoring the rules but told myself that nothing would happen to the bear man; besides I would never get caught.

I did not plan to hike all the way to the plateau, just go a short distance along it, until I spotted some bears. After convincing myself that my actions were justified, I began walking up the restricted trail, using extreme caution. My good intentions came to naught, however; five hours later, I was still on the trail and still searching for bears. Just then, a helicopter appeared, hovered overhead for a few moments, then came in for a landing. I was caught "bear-handed."

A park warden clambered out of the aircraft; he did not appear to be amused. "You are hiking in a closed area," he told me shortly. "I am required to remove you." The pilot, on the other hand, made light of the incident, asking if I had hiked in the closed area to get a free helicopter ride. The warden did not even crack a smile as he informed me that I was going to be charged with hiking in a closed area, and that I would be required to appear in court.

A few days later, I arrived at the courthouse to argue my case. I pleaded not guilty and attempted to explain that I was not hiking in the closed section, but in the nearby hills. My defence was weak, and everyone knew it. Before giving his decision on my fate later that afternoon, the judge grinned and asked me if I thought I was outnumbered by park wardens, and I had to agree—the prosecution consisted of twelve wardens, and I was the only one on my side.

At that point, the warden who had arrested me took over. "Was I trying to commit suicide by hiking in an area infested with grizzlies?" he wondered. In retrospect, his question was rather comical, but I could see that he was seriously concerned. I told him no, I was not attempting suicide, I was just trying to get some good bear pictures. The warden did not respond sympathetically. As the park attendant had told me, he said, eight grizzlies had recently been seen near where I had been hiking and despite my feeble arguments, I had in fact been hiking in the closed section—indeed, at the time of my capture, I was not far from the plateau itself. I momentarily considered pleading insanity, but I assumed that was already clear.

The judge found me guilty as charged and asked the arresting warden what sentence should be imposed on me. After a short recess, the warden, now smiling, asked the judge to order that I show my bear program, free of charge, in the communities of Destruction Bay and Haines Junction. More to the point, I should be required to keep the peace. The judge agreed, and

I did as I was told. I have always been grateful that the wardens and the judge were good sports.

I later returned to the park and was pleased to find out that Sheep Bullion Plateau was now open to hikers. I packed my gear and immediately set off on a hike. After several hours, I reached the open meadows and soon encountered a grizzly sow with two yearling cubs, feeding on the protein-rich grass that is characteristic of vegetation at high elevations.

I kept a safe distance from the dining bears and watched. The mother bear was being very protective, and she never wandered farther than nine meters from the cubs. This is common behaviour: a sow is particularly solicitous of cubs that are less than a year old. After getting a few good pictures, I decided it was time to leave.

Rams fighting.

The next morning, I returned to the same area and spotted a grizzly boar—or perhaps I should say he spotted me, because he was standing right in front of me, ten metres away, staring into my eyes. I looked right back at him, but the bear won the staring contest; defeated, I slowly turned to my right and began to hike away at a cautious pace. The grizzly continued to stare. When I was about twenty-four metres from the bear, I breathed a sigh of relief believing that I was now much safer. Indeed, the bear no longer felt threatened, and he wandered away, across a nearby hill. As I walked across the same hillside, I came upon a fox, and he too watched me closely as I passed.

Sheep Bullion Plateau is one of the most beautiful places I have ever visited; the scenery is breathtaking. There are no trees, and the green alpine meadows extend in every direction, as far as the eye can see. I am uncertain if bears enjoy scenery, but I suspect they do. I *am* sure that they

The meadows of Sheep Bullion Plateau.

enjoy the grasses and roots that grow in abundance throughout the plateau; however, their diet is not exclusively vegetarian and this area is also the home of Arctic ground squirrels, moose, and dall sheep. After the main course, the bear must consider dessert: in late summer and fall, the valleys are full of berries, which make a fine sequel to a meal of roots or meat. It is no wonder that bears choose to live in mountainous regions.

During the summer of 1994, I went to Mount Edziza in northern British Columbia. It is an isolated wilderness area west of Kinaskan Lake and is accessible if you are willing to hike for ten hours. The one village is Telegraph Creek. The hike is a combination of knee-deep mud and thick forest, a condition my friend Jim could really appreciate. Only the flies were missing. The only relief from the mud was the ice-cold streams that I had to wade across.

About halfway to Mount Edziza the rain started coming down making the conditions even worse. There were plenty of bear signs including tracks and recent droppings. The rain was making the trail impassable so I decided to set up my tent on the side of the rapid running Chakima Creek. Because of the bear activity I strung a fishing line around my tent so that if a bear stumbled into it, my fishing reel would make a noise alerting me to the intruder. With the alarm set, I tried to get some sleep.

I had my first visitor before the sun came up. A bear cub began whining outside my tent. Normally bears are quiet but this bear was probably disturbed by the close proximity of my tent. The guttural grunts lasted a few moments until I hit a pot with a spoon and the woods returned to silence. I slept the rest of the night with one eye and both ears open. The next morning I was granted relief from the rain and I continued pushing my way through the mud. The trail became steeper the farther I went and less defined as the trees thinned out. Instead of a clear path of mud it was now a large field of mud.

On every trip I seem to take at least one wrong turn, and this trip was no different. I mistakenly got lost, which is understandable considering every direction provided the same view—mud. I ended up at a spectacular waterfall with small trout trying to overcome the rapids below it. I doubt anyone else has ever been to this spot.

Finally I got my bearings. In the distance I spotted what I thought were volcanic rocks so I began walking in that direction. I found several animal trails that circumnavigated the mud and made walking much easier. When I reached the rocks I was surprised to see they were sitting on large piles of volcanic sand like buoys floating on the sea. The sand was light brown and very fine, the rocks a burnt colour. Small deposits of yellow, blue, and pink flowers were growing randomly in the sand. Streams, originating from patches of ice and snow, peppered the landscape and continually moved the sand, although tracks of caribou and mountain goats could be distinguished at shallow crossing points. The volcanic craters were five kilometres away, and I was surprised at the great distance the volcanic rocks had been thrown.

I spent some time searching for bears but there were no tracks or signs. The closest thing I found was a goat skull laying on the side of a hill. The sunsets made up for the lack of bears and for all the mud.

After leaving Mount Edziza I went to Fish Creek for my yearly visit. After a short hike I came upon a three-year-old brown grizzly that had just arrived at the creek. When a bear first arrives at Fish Creek it appears very excited. This particular bear was soon dashing from side to side pursuing the scattering delicacies. Next, he dove into the water, grabbed a salmon, brought it to shore and began to eat it. Soon the bear was walking in my direction but he was not threatening; he simply wanted access to the bear path that was on the other side of me. I went a few metres off the trail and watched the bear depart.

As I was walking down a trail a week later, a black bear approached me. I backed up slowly, but the bear kept coming. Obviously the young bear had not heard the old rule of leaving when something did not pose a threat. Preparing for the worst, I picked up my tripod and positioned it in the bear's path. The bear was a juvenile grizzly and they are often extremely inquisitive. When he was within range, I lowered the tripod and tapped him on the head. It was not a hard strike but it was enough to startle the bear and he retreated in the opposite direction.

Grizzly feeding on a salmon carcass.

It was also during this trip that I watched a brown bear swimming in a pond near Fish Creek. So much for the myth that bears cannot swim; they are, in fact, good swimmers, as this particular bear proved. He dove underwater and retreived a dead salmon from the bottom of the pond—an easy meal.

started my usual routine of talking loudly to scare away whatever was out there. My imagination was running wild, as I pictured myself quarrelling with, then being devoured by, the King Kong of grizzly bears. But all was quiet, and I slept peacefully for the rest of the night.

At dawn, I got up and had a look around near my campsite. Close to the tent, I came upon one of the largest grizzly tracks I have ever seen, longer and wider than my own foot. Briefly I imagined an elephant with claws until I remembered that track must have been left by last night's visitor. I considered running for the safety of the village, but then I had visions of getting a picture of this monstrous bear.

I nervously picked my way along the trail, heading in the direction of the Karluk River. Along the way, I saw a small brook-fed pond where innumerable small fish were jumping; there seemed to be a hundred of them in the air at any given moment. I was uncertain if they were trout or salmon, but it was quite something to behold. A few kilometres farther was a less-welcome sight—a big patch of bog—which I reluctantly waded through as there was no turning back!

I arrived at the Karluk River in which many chum salmon and silver salmon splashed as they swam upstream. There were several dead salmon along the riverbank, and knowing how much grizzlies enjoy salmon, I began to move very slowly and cautiously; these fish had been caught by bears, partially eaten, then discarded. The tastiest portions of the salmon—including the skin, brain, and roe—had been consumed. There were no grizzlies in sight, but I had a

The grizzly bear.

Grizzly paw print.

feeling they were nearby. With all this food swimming around, they would certainly be back.

Several bald eagles were flying overhead, dipping down to dine on the leftover fish. I watched the majestic birds and waited around for a few hours, but the only other animals I saw were three deer that had wandered out of the forest to have a drink in the river. They waded out in the water for only a moment, though, then nervously looked in the direction they had come from and sprang away. I tried to figure out what was worrying them, and although nothing else emerged from the dense underbrush, I had an odd feeling that something was lurking back there, just out of sight.

I decided to continue hiking, trying to be quiet but unable to keep the branches and twigs from rustling and snapping as I moved. Maybe I would do better to try out the bear trail that ran beside the river, so I returned to the area where the deer had been drinking. As I scanned the brush, I suddenly noticed the rear end of a grizzly; it was so big that I blinked to reassure myself that I wasn't hallucinating. If this was the back, I was scared to see the front; in fact, of all the rumps I have ever observed—and I have seen some big ones—this was the largest. Imagine a furry Toyota, and you will have a good idea of this bear's backside. I considered taking a picture, but perhaps it was unwise to "expose" impressionable school children to such a spectacle. Before I could make up my mind, the bear started moving away and, despite its size, I could not see where it was going. Just then, the bushes began to rattle to my right. Could this bear be circling me?

Fearing the worst, I went down to the river and waded into the cold water, heading upstream and glancing back every few moments to see if I were being followed. No signs of the bear anywhere. After wading in the water for about ten minutes, I felt safe, so I rejoined the trail back to Larsen Bay, questioning my sanity as I hiked. What was I trying to prove by hiking alone without any protection, especially in an area where the bears were bigger than houses?

I had made up my mind to return to the village when I saw several deer dart away from a meadow where they had been grazing; just ahead of me were two brown-and-white foxes that had apparently caused the disturbance. Seeing these less dangerous animals restored my courage; I became more determined than ever to get some good bear photos. I would continue hiking towards Larsen Bay, but I would search carefully for a promising spot to see bears. I even felt bold enough to plan to camp that night. As I neared the community, I noticed a stream full of pink salmon. This abundance made for a prime bear-watching spot. Grizzly tracks were everywhere, and two bear trails led out of the thicket and down towards the stream. One of the paths had been used so frequently that it was padded down like a dirt road.

Early the next morning I was safely ensconced in a lookout tree near the stream when a light-brown grizzly sow, maybe weighing one hundred kilograms, wandered out of the bush and walked over to the stream. She lost no time getting her breakfast—a single lunge into the water, and she emerged with a small, bright salmon in her mouth. Obviously famished, she returned to shore and ferociously tore the fish to pieces, ignoring the pesky magpies flying overhead and occasionally landing nearby, waiting for leftovers. The fish was soon devoured and the grizzly returned to the stream, where she sat down to cool herself in the icy water; she rolled in it and thrashed around, then stood up and shook herself dry. Eventually, she caught another fish and carried it into the woods. This was a good start; I was glad to get some pictures—from the safety of my lookout tree.

A few uneventful days passed, and finally my patience was rewarded: on the third evening, two chocolate-brown grizzlies emerged from one of the trails, each about 275 kilograms. It was too dark to get any decent photographs, but I was thrilled to see those enormous bears.

It was another couple of days before the sound of snapping twigs in the woods signalled the presence of another bear—this one a silver-tipped grizzly wandering along one of the bear trails. I was surprised by its colour, because most grizzlies on the island, at least those living within eighty kilometres of the coastline, are dark or light brown. But there are always some exceptions, as this magnificent bear proved.

The following week, the weather turned cold. The grass and leaves were tinged with yellow, and the cold wind blew in with a vengeance. One morning, as I approached my leafy lookout, I was startled by the sound of scratching. To my amazement, I saw a full-grown grizzly clambering up a cottonwood tree about sixty metres away. Nor did he ascend a little way and then drop back down; this bear climbed more than six metres before he reached the first limbs, where he stopped to rest.

I was also surprised to see how easily he climbed, shifting his enormous bulk with considerable grace and hugging the tree with his paws as he went. Park officials have always claimed that adult grizzlies cannot climb trees, because their front claws are too long and not curved enough. Didn't this bear realize he couldn't climb?

As the bear sat there looking around, I got so excited about recording this extraordinary sight on film that I ran towards his perch— just in time to see another grizzly boar come out of the bushes near the tree, heading in my direction. I stopped, stood my ground, and hoped the bear would not become overwrought and charge me. That would be like being attacked by a tank—this grizzly weighed over 455 kilograms, more than three times as much as the one up the tree. When he got within ten metres of me, he stopped, turned in the opposite direction, and lumbered over to the other side of the tree, where he stared up at the grizzly sitting high above us.

Grizzly boar approaching.

I realized that the large boar had been chasing the smaller bear, which might have inadvertently wandered into his pursuer's territory. But I don't think the bigger grizzly was expecting the intruder to come up with quite the escape route he chose. I'm not sure which of us was more amazed—me or the enormous bear at the base of the cottonwood.

I tried to move to a better position for taking photographs, but my movements prompted the boar to shift his attention from the treed grizzly to me. I didn't think my heart could survive another approach from this huge creature, so I kept still, and he went back to watching the other bear. We all waited for about ten minutes for something to happen; all the while, I was vigorously snapping pictures. Finally, the large boar stood up, shot me a parting glance, and wandered away, disappearing into the dense vegetation.

With his antagonist out of the way, the treed grizzly focused on me. I reacted to the disapproving look by slowly backing away from the tree, and he began climbing down. He descended rump first, with his paws hugging the tree—not a particularly elegant sight, but effective climbing just the same. At the bottom, he stood on his hind legs, put his front paws against the tree, and had a good look at me. He seemed to be grinning, although it may have been my imagination. After a moment, the bear dropped down on all fours and quickly wandered away.

This unusual experience made it difficult for me to sleep for several nights, but I stayed in the area in the hopes of seeing those bears again. Early one afternoon, I spotted the large boar sleeping on the side of a bear trail, not far from where we had met previously. I watched him for a while, keeping well back; occasionally, he lifted his head and sniffed the air, then went back to sleep. After about forty minutes, the bear rose and casually walked away—a much tamer encounter than our earlier meeting.

The weather was getting extremely bad, so I headed back to Larsen Bay. When I got to the village grocery store, a lady asked me if I was "the bear man." I was uncertain why she was using that term, but I replied that, yes, I did enjoy photographing and studying bears. Apparently, news of my hobby was widespread, and several other residents approached me to

Grizzly backing down a tree.

Grizzly checking out the area.

inquire about the bear sightings I had made. I heard the term "bear man" from the villagers quite frequently, and I thought it was funny, and it was only later, as I was about to board the plane home, that I discovered that the joke was on me. To my great embarrassment, I realized the entire rear end of my pants had been torn away. I had been wandering around town with my underwear in plain view. I wondered if they really meant "*bare* man," rather than "bear man"; I guess both terms fit.

As I left the area I was glad that I had come. Despite the rugged terrain, I had managed to get some incredible photographs, including the rare image of an adult grizzly up a tree. And I had seen what surely must qualify among the world's largest buttocks.

10

Fish Creek, Alaska

Hiking In Bear Country

Fish Creek, Hyder, Alaska

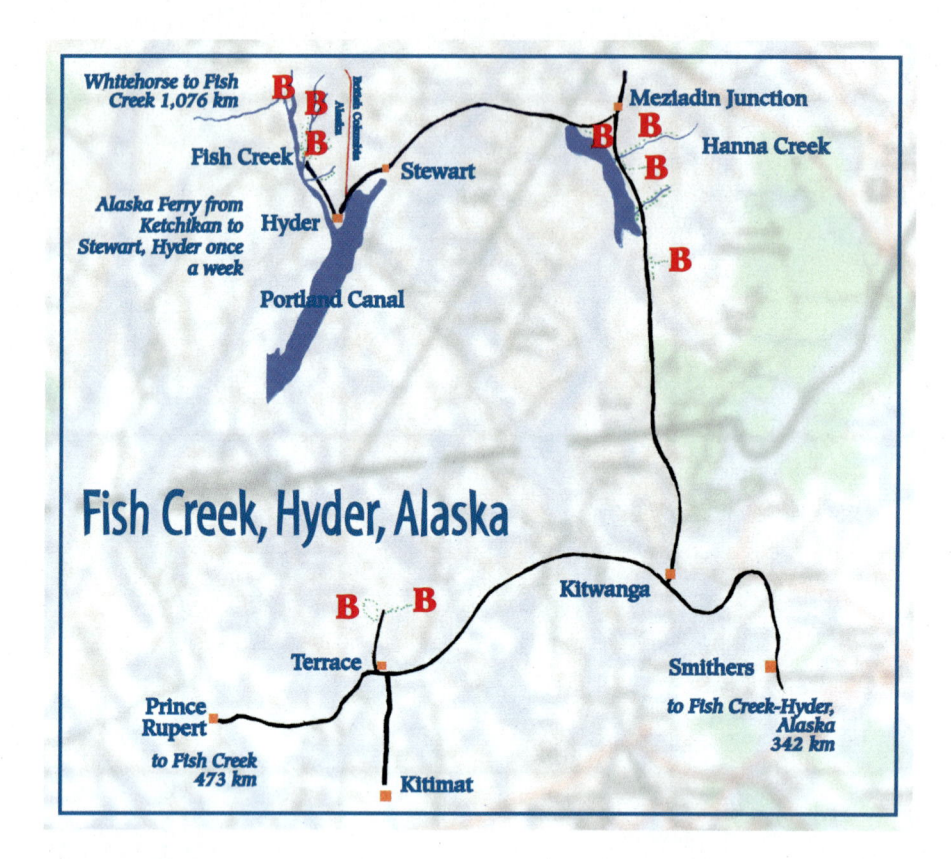

The Fish Creek bear sanctuary is located across the border from Stewart, British Columbia, about eight kilometres from the village of Hyder, Alaska (population ninety). The village is located near the mouth of the Salmon River and is surrounded by several large green mountains, a few of which are snow-capped.

The sanctuary is renowned for the many salmon that spawn in its rivers and streams, attracting hungry black bears and grizzlies. Because the bears are protected, they thrive here; in fact, the bear population is so large that the residents of Hyder are used to seeing both grizzlies and black bears roaming through their streets at night. Normally, the mixture of bears and people is not a happy one for either species, but Hyder is a special place, where they coexist quite peacefully.

This was not always the case. One of the local experts on Hyder, an information officer, has told me about several shocking incidents that took place in the early days of Hyder. These stories all had a common theme: human cruelty towards bears. Indeed, most of the stories ended with a bear being shot for fun. I am always sad to hear about these kinds of incidents, but the saddest part of all is that I have become accustomed to hearing about people's many acts of unkindness.

I decided to take a day off from searching for bears and visited nearby Salmon Glacier, one of the largest in the world, and well worth seeing. At the "toe" of the glacier is Tide Lake, which is really a part-time lake formed in winter as ice accumulates and creates a dam that prevents any water from escaping. The water's silty white colour makes it an unusual sight. As the weather becomes warmer, the dam eventually breaks and the water flows towards Fish Creek and Salmon River.

Once the water has left Tide Lake, the icebergs that were once floating now sit on dry land, and one can easily walk among them. Some of these stranded icebergs are enormous, and when walking near them that day, I would constantly look up in case any big chunks were about to break off.

Searching for bears has led me to some very strange places, and this is one of them. The eerie landscape perfectly fits my idea of science fiction.

Having spent an afternoon among the glaciers, it was time to get back to the bear business, so I returned to Hyder.

The residents of Hyder are very conscious of bear safety. Cyclists carry a can of bear spray for protection, while local wardens always have a shotgun close by when they go out tagging fish. Some tourists are allowed to carry a rifle when hiking or fishing but must shoot above a bear to scare it away; during an attack, however, they can shoot to kill. It normally bothers me when people carry guns in areas where there are bears, but after speaking to local employees of the fish and wildlife service, I understand their position.

The wildlife officers explained that they love bears as much as I do, but there is always a chance that a bear may get aggressive. The shotguns

Salmon Glacier.

are used to scare the bears and are only fired in the air. They did acknowledge, however, that they would shoot an attacking bear; luckily this has never happened. Indeed, they have become so familiar with the bears at Fish Creek that they have given nicknames to many of the most frequent visitors—Harold, Mahogany, Shadow, Sugar Sow, Brown Pants, Big Ears, and the local favourite, Festus, who was injured in a hunting accident and now walks with a limp.

Fish Creek is the Promised Land for anyone that appreciates nature. Gulls and bald eagles continually fly over the creeks, and below them the salmon splash and struggle against the current. This habitat is filled with sound, and the noise creates a wonderful symphony. It is amazing to watch fish during the spawning period, and each time I see this process, I appreciate life a little more.

Three species of salmon spawn in Fish Creek: chum salmon, or dogfish; pink salmon, also called humpbacks; and coho, also known as silver salmon. These fish remain at sea for several years, then instinctively return to their birthplace to continue the cycle of life, laying thousands of eggs and guarding them as long as they can. Normally, salmon die within ten days of spawning; dead salmon in a stream can be a sad sight, but it helps to remember that in a few months, thousands of new salmon will be thriving in these waters.

It is immediately apparent to a visitor why bears along the Kodiak Island coastline are so large and magnificent. From July to November, coastal bears can eat all the salmon they want; this rich food causes the bears to gain weight quickly. Inland bears are also beautiful, but because they do not eat as much salmon, they are not nearly as large.

My visit to the area took place in August, and there were plenty of chum salmon spawning in Fish Creek. I hiked along the shore, occasionally glancing at the water to watch the salmon swimming upstream. On the shoreline were several decaying fish carcasses—a repulsive smell, as far as humans are concerned, but judging from the reaction of birds and bears, it must have some delightful qualities. For me, the sight of rotting fish is a signal to take a wide detour.

Jim Kahl among the icebergs on one of our trips together to Hyder.

The noise along that shoreline was continuous; slapping, splattering, and splashing of the salmon drowned out any sounds that nearby birds or animals might be making. I knew there were bears in the area, so I tried to be much more aware of any activity out of the ordinary. Of course, when you are this far from civilization, everything seems out of the ordinary.

I continued walking until I approached an area with shallow spawning beds, where I could easily see the backs of chum salmon sticking out of the water, only about five centimetres deep. On the other side of the stream, I noticed two bear tunnels among some bushes; these distinctive passages are well-used trails that go through very thick brush and are often covered with brush at the 1.2 metre level. The ones I saw appeared to extend approximately thirty metres into the shadows of the brush. If I were patient, there was a good chance that a bear would eventually come out of one of these tunnels; with this in mind, I decided to hike nearby.

Resting salmon.

Scouting around for a good lookout spot, I came upon a bear trail on the shore that led from the creek to the tunnels, both sides of which were littered with fish remains, likely discarded by bears. To compensate for splashing noises coming from the creek, I would move for a few moments, then pause to listen for any large animals that might be nearby. I had to be especially careful when I approached turns, not knowing what could be lurking around each bend.

I was still within sight of the bear tunnels, and had just been listening intently for a very long moment, when I was suddenly confronted by a bear. My ears are evidently not what they used to be, although my ways of thinking remain the same. Perhaps this was my problem. In any case, the black bear was only about eight metres away. He began to walk towards me, so I responded by talking to him: "I'm right in front of you." He hesitated, then kept on coming. I was running out of options, so I pointed my tripod at him and, in a gruff voice, said, "Don't come any closer." The bear stopped again. Maybe he understood me; possibly he was just not hungry enough to eat me—whatever his reasons, he turned and waded across the creek, up an embankment, and into a bear tunnel, where he disappeared. What a close call! I suddenly felt quite sick, and it took me several moments to recover before I continued down the stream, pointing my tripod in front of me in the hopes that my luck would hold.

Early that evening, while watching Fish Creek, I caught sight of a young black bear emerging from the bushes. He was probably quite young—he weighed only about fifty-four kilograms—and had likely been chased away by his mother within the last few months. He was still learning how to survive on his own, which became all too clear when he went down to the water and began to chase salmon. After a few unsuccessful attempts, he settled for one of the dead chum salmon lying along the shoreline.

As the small bear was eating his aged salmon, he was disturbed by a noise to his rear: a large boar came out of the woods. This black bear weighed close to 135 kilograms—one of the largest I've ever seen—and he clearly did not appreciate the small bear helping himself to what he viewed as his property. Without hesitation, he hopped across Fish Creek and darted into the woods. The boar followed for a few minutes, but then turned back to the creek—and a meal.

It did not take long for the boar to plunge his head into the water and emerge with a large chum salmon clenched in his jaws. He was so close that I could have touched him—although I did not feel tempted—and his beady brown eyes were on me, as water trickled off his fur and the salmon occasionally twitched between his teeth. My heart skipped a beat as the bear looked me over for a very long moment, then turned around and, with the fish still in his mouth, made his way to the other side of Fish Creek.

When the bear reached the opposite shoreline, he placed the salmon down, held it between his paws, then started to eat. Within a few minutes, most of the fish was gone; only the head and tail remained. Bears in the Fish Creek area will eat the top portion of a salmon head, the egg sacks, and the salmon's body. The tail and the face of the salmon are usually discarded, even by the hungriest of bears. In fact, their taste in fish is similar to my own, although I like to clean mine first.

Having finished off his first salmon, the black bear returned to the creek and caught a second one. This bear was hungry, and the fish soon vanished. While he was eating, no other bears came near, and they were wise to avoid him. Nothing was going to come between him and his salmon. If another bear had strayed into the area, he would not have lingered; the larger a bear, the more dominant and territorial he is—and this was one big, tough-looking adversary. I certainly would not want to quarrel with him.

Large black bear charging a smaller bear.

This was turning out to be an excellent day for getting photos, and the big bear cooperated by striking many fine poses. But he was not my only model. In the distance, I caught sight of a light-coloured cinnamon bear, which wandered over to the shoreline, quickly caught a salmon, then returned to the forest. Luckily for him, the huge boar was too intent on his fishing to notice the interloper. Cinnamon-coloured black bears, which can be either light or dark, are more commonly found west of the Rockies, so sighting this bear was not that unusual.

I began to hike downstream, and as I walked, there was a scratching sound on a nearby tree. Halfway up was a black bear cub, staring down at me. There is a well-known bear proverb: "Where there is a cub, there is also a mother bear nearby." Therefore, I was cautious and did not make any sudden movements.

After about ten minutes had passed, the mother bear appeared and walked within about four metres of my position before heading towards Fish Creek. With another bear proverb in mind—"Never disturb a mother bear"—I remained still. Within a few moments, the sow had caught a chum salmon and was coming back towards my position.

It was at this point that I remembered the most important bear proverb of all: "Do not get eaten by a bear." I shuffled my feet until I was hidden behind a tree. When the mother arrived at the base of the tree where her cub was waiting up in the branches, she dropped the salmon, and uttered a low, grunting noise—the bear equivalent of "Supper is ready." The cub responded by climbing down. As the proverbs suggest, it is dangerous for a human to be near a mother bear and her cub at any time, but it is an even worse idea to do so when they are eating because bears are extremely protective of their food. I did not want to become part of their meal, nor did I want to disturb them, so I cautiously moved away.

I had walked for only a minute in the direction of the stream when I noticed some bushes rustling on the opposite shore. Directly across from me, yet another black bear came out of the bushes and walked down to the water. This bear was an unusual colour—coal black, except for his legs, which were brown. I later learned this was a very well known bear, recognized locally as Brown Pants.

I slowly sat down in an attempt not to disturb Brown Pants, who was standing right in front of me, but he was utterly disinterested in my presence. There were fish to catch, and his gaze was fixed on the stream. Suddenly, he jumped forward, causing water to splash in every direction, and emerged with a salmon. After eating his snack, Brown Pants continued walking upstream, looking for a main course, but he wasn't having much luck and had to settle for some salmon eggs, which he licked up from the bottom of the stream bed. He was soon out of sight, and this was a disappointment; watching him fish had been quite entertaining. Just after Brown Pants left, another black bear came out of the brush and I got a shot of him licking

Bear with salmon.

salmon eggs of the stream bottom.

I then set up my hammock on a nearby tree and tried, unsuccessfully, to go to sleep. Bears were splashing around in the water all night, and it was not particularly restful to contemplate the close proximity of these hungry animals. At the same time, it was a remarkable experience to see the shadows of the bears dance in the moonlight.

At noon the next day, a black bear sow with two yearling cubs appeared on the shoreline of the creek. Considering she had two cubs, this sow was small. But she proved to be an excellent provider. Ignoring the loud splashing of the salmon, the mother bear wandered into the middle of the stream, while the cubs sat down on the rocky shoreline and watched patiently. With a sudden burst of energy, the sow ran down the centre of the creek, stopped, then plunged her head into the water, pulling out a large chum salmon. Next, she waded out of the stream and led her cubs into the woods. The salmon that had been stirred up by the intruding bear returned to their spawning beds, and within a few moments, the creek was once again calm.

Cinnamon black bear.

Black bear catching salmon.

It took the sow and her cubs five minutes at most to devour the salmon, after which they returned to the creek. The mother bear made a low grunting sound, and the cubs obediently sat down. After a few moments of intense focus on the water, she jumped into the creek, causing a commotion among the salmon. Indeed, the splashing mounted a panicked frenzy. But the sow was indifferent to the plight of her future dinner, and after several quick, graceful movements, she emerged with another salmon. The second helping firmly gripped between her jaws, she returned to the woods, her family close behind.

About ten minutes later, they were back. I began to wonder just how hungry these bears were—and whether she would mind catching one of those salmon for me. But I was out of luck: the three bears were headed across the creek. About halfway to the other side, one of the cubs playfully tried to snag a salmon. The young bear's attempt was futile, and I could relate to his disappointment.

Black bear cub waiting for mom.

On the opposite side of the creek, the other cub picked up a dead salmon and shook it between his jaws, imitating the movements of his mother after she had caught a fish. Perhaps this was the secret to successful fishing—imitating someone who knows how. After a few moments, the cub dropped the fish in some bushes, and the family wandered out of sight.

I was pleased at having witnessed this fishing lesson, and my attention quickly turned to the stream. I noticed several pink salmon swimming along with the chum salmon; not only did the local bears have volume, they also had variety. Fish Creek is relatively small—three metres across at the place where I was standing—but it contains thousands upon thousands of salmon at spawning time. Every section of the creek was saturated by masses of fish. Even I should be able to catch something amid this abundance, but it was late and I had the excuse of being tired. That night I heard several bears feeding in the creek. It was another moonlit night, and once again I delighted in the magic of their shadows leaping on the water. I was startled when one bear walked directly beneath my hammock on his way to the creek. He may have smelled me, because he stopped as he passed, then grunted and stood on his hind legs before dropping back down on all fours and making his way towards the creek. Needless to say, it was another very long night.

Black bear licking up salmon eggs.

    At dawn the next day, a large boar cautiously made his way along the stream and towards me. But about twenty metres away, he stopped, picked up a dead salmon, then returned to the woods. I had a feeling the bear had not gone very far to have breakfast, so I waited and kept a close eye on the nearby trees. After a period of silence, I said a brief prayer, climbed down from my tree, and walked along the shoreline.

    This was turning out to be an unusually productive bear-sighting expedition. I had gone only a short distance when I spotted a grizzly sow with a seven-month-old cub, standing on the shore of the creek. This sow was unusually thin and appeared to be in poor physical condition; the hump on her shoulders was extremely prominent, further indication that she was not eating well or was sick. The bear also seemed very nervous, yet another sign of illness or poor nutrition. Realizing this, I stood very still. The two bears approached me, but as they sensed my presence, they quickly moved away and into the woods.

Three days later, I spotted the infamous bear known to the locals as Big Ears. The name fit. This grizzly had enormous ears and a big grizzly grin. He looked like an evil clown, but in point of fact he was just a thin young grizzly that had recently been left on his own and who would have to learn how to catch fish much more adeptly if he expected to gain any stature in his community.

Now that the bear was closer, his features didn't seem quite so odd. Besides, who was I to take issue with his appearance? I probably seemed just as peculiar-looking to him. Big Ears grinned at me, then started to chew on a dead salmon that was lying between us. Occasionally, he would smile and watch me, and during

Big Ears.

those moments I wondered what he was thinking. Once, I even thought I heard him laugh. After a few moments, Big Ears walked away and began to eat some blueberries that were growing on a nearby hillside.

That night, I set up my tent near Fish Creek. It was after midnight when I woke up and realized that a bear was just outside my tent. I remained motionless, and after a few moments of silence, I checked outside—there was the shadow of a large bear, moving away. As always, I felt a little nervous to see such an ominous sight, but what could I do? I returned to my sleeping bag and loudly discussed my genuine love of all forest creatures. This tactic normally puts every living thing in the vicinity to sleep, including myself; it didn't fail this time. The next morning, I woke unharmed—the ideal way to start a day.

My backpack, however, had fared much more poorly—the bear had climbed the tree where I had hung it. He must have been a very clever bear, because he somehow untied a rope that I had strung between two trees. And he must have been fussy, because all he ate was a single chocolate bar.

With my backpack only a wee bit lighter, I continued hiking. The odour of dead salmon was extremely strong along the shoreline, and several bald eagles flew overhead, searching for snacks. Some of the birds had dark feathers on their heads, which indicated that they were less than four years old; when eagles reach four years of age, the feathers on their heads turn white. After taking pictures of the birds, I noticed two grizzlies walk down a nearby hillside, stopping frequently to sniff the dead salmon along the shoreline.

Black bear preparing to jump.

These grizzlies were not very interested in the aged carcasses and instead went out into the water, where they began to feed on the live salmon. Unlike me, the grizzlies both caught a fish on every try, their movements lightening-fast.

The bears would rush forward and dive into the water. When their heads reappeared, a fish would be dangling below each bear's nostrils. Next, the bear would adjust the flapping fish with its paws to get a better grip, and with a sudden crunch of the bear's teeth the fish would go limp. After carrying the salmon to shore, the bear would quickly devour his catch.

These bears caught and ate fish after fish without any trouble; their fishing experience was paying off in the form of a huge feast. The abilities of these grizzlies—and their large size—reinforced the notion that some bears catch and eat as many as thirty fish a day.

One of the two grizzlies was a sow, who fished in a crisscross pattern that eventually brought her in my direction. When she was about six metres away, she noticed me, and must have been startled at my intrusive presence, because she immediately lowered her head and started towards me. The gap between us was quickly closing, but the sow continued to charge, with the bristles of her furry back sticking straight up. I was not sure what this meant, but it was probably not a good sign.

Three metres from where I was standing, the grizzly stopped and stared at me. I did not move, except to talk to her in as calm a voice as I could muster. "Don't come any closer; I don't want to hurt you," I said. "Just leave me alone, and I won't bother you." I repeated this nonsense three times—as if I were any match for a grizzly bear!—and luckily the bear returned to the creek, where she was soon feasting on salmon again.

I retreated for a quick change of pants, and, with my clothes dry and my pride wounded, I continued to watch the two bears. The sow was having extremely good luck at catching salmon, and this seemed to bother the boar. He watched her catch a fish, then he walked over and tried to steal it. The two grizzlies gripped the fish in their teeth, and soon a tug of war broke out. This apparently did nothing to resolve the dispute, because the bears soon forgot all about the fish and began wrestling each other. The match was terrific, especially when the contenders stood on their hind legs, trying to box each other with their front paws. The bout lasted for five or so minutes and ended in a draw. Soon the two nutty grizzlies settled down and waded back into the creek.

Young bald eagle.

After a brief rest, both grizzlies stood up on their hind legs again and stared upstream. They must have been disturbed by something, because they suddenly dropped down on all fours and darted across the creek and

Two grizzlies.

A charging grizzly.

into the woods. About ten minutes passed, and then a large cinnamon bear emerged from the woods, grabbed one of the dead salmon and returned to the woods. A while later, the same bear returned, and this time I spotted a cub at her side. This sow was being cautious with her foraging, in order to protect the cub from other bears that might be in the same area. The two wrestling grizzlies had probably smelled her coming and decided to avoid a confrontation. The cinnamon bear grabbed another fish, then she and her cub disappeared into the bushes.

The next day, I was standing on a rock beside the creek when two grizzlies came out of the woods behind me. One of the bears was a sow, and she walked to within three metres of my position, then stopped and stared in my direction. I began to talk in a low voice: "Don't come any closer. Leave me alone." The other bear, a boar, closed in to about four metres away from me—but he was obviously unconcerned about my presence, because he stood on his hind legs and began to eat some berries off a tall bush. Within a few moments, both grizzlies had left my side and gone fishing, about five metres away. The bears were easily catching fish with even more ease than the quarrelling couple had because the spawning salmon in this part of the stream were extremely weak and close to death.

These bears were unique among those I saw during my visit. Every day, for the rest of that week, they would return to the same fishing spot. There, late in the afternoon, they would begin a ritual. After helping themselves to several salmon from the stream, they wrestled for a while, becoming more and more playful until they were gently batting at each other with light, delicate flicks of their paws.

These bears provided not only some excellent entertainment, but also a number of great photographs. Soon, however, the days became extremely short, and the rainy season began. It was time to leave this magical place.

An awkward position.

The following summer, I returned to the area to watch the bears again, and was devastated by the news that one of the two playful grizzlies I had been photographing the previous summer had been shot. Possibly the bear had surprised a poacher or a fisherman carrying a rifle. If so, the "sportsman" didn't report the incident. Several of the residents described how the grizzly's body had laid rotting in the creek for several weeks. What a terrible waste!

I was also surprised to see only one black bear during the two weeks I spent around Hyder Creek, which is usually swarming with bears. There were several rumours in town that attempted to explain the diminishing black bear population, the strongest of which claimed that the bears had been shot as they entered the dump area of nearby Stewart, British Columbia. On the Alaskan side of the border, they are protected by the bear sanctuary, but as soon as they walk into Canada, they become easy targets. I was told that during the previous fall, as many as forty-seven bears had been killed.

The news of the mass killing of bears was shocking, and I wanted to do something about it. A good friend of mine, who is also a bear enthusiast, made inquiries of the fish and wildlife officers in Smithers (a town 337 kilometres southeast of Hyder), attempting to find out exactly how many bears had been shot, and why. They told my friend they would look into it and give her a call back, but they never did.

I then launched a petition asking the Canadian government to extend the Alaskan bear sanctuary into Canada far enough to protect most of the bear population. The form was widely circulated throughout the Fish Creek-Hyder area, and signed by people from Germany, England, France, Australia, and throughout North America. A large group of French tourists was particularly miffed; they had come to the area to see bears, but after four days of searching, they had still not seen any. One of the petitioners summed up the situation by saying: "These bears should be protected on both sides of the border because the bears are the main reason that tourists come to the Stewart–Hyder area. By not protecting the bears, we are not protecting the insurgence of tourist dollars."

Beyond the economic impact of the bears, there is also a moral issue that should be considered. One must weigh the importance of protecting bears against the barbaric satisfaction derived by those who shoot bears for enjoyment. There will always be people who see nothing wrong with inflicting needless suffering on animals, but perhaps through education some of these individuals can be converted into citizens who respect life in all its forms.

Many people are in dire need of such education, and I have had the

Arguing grizzlies.

Grizzlies sniffing dead salmon.

misfortune of meeting some of them. One man, for example, bragged to me that he had shot twenty-two bears the previous fall, and he challenged me to do something about it. When I encounter such people, I ask myself why they behave in such a way. Could it be that they have such miserable lives that they can only get pleasure by watching something suffer? Clearly, some people will require more help than others.

Nevertheless, my petition did represent a significant number of people, and in August 1993 I attempted to draw further attention to our concerns by picketing in front of the British Columbia environment office. Within half an hour, I was invited to attend a meeting with the director and four fish and wildlife officers. During the half-hour meeting, the officials explained that in the previous year, they only took part in the shootings of two bears in the Stewart area that were killed because they were in very poor condition. The only other activity in which the office was involved was the trapping of eighteen bears slated for relocation.

I was pleased to hear that the bears I thought had been killed may simply have been moved. The many bear carcasses that were sighted at the Stewart dump had probably been left there by poachers, who often kill the animals to further black-market sales of bears' bladders, prized for their medicinal qualities by many Asian cultures.

At the meeting, I was informed that an electric fence had been built around the Stewart dump as part of a joint effort between the town of Stewart and the British Columbia government. Since the fence has been built, several bears have been seen trying to get past the fence; they receive a mild shock then leave unharmed. The fence serves a dual purpose: it denies poachers easy access to bears that come to the dump and discourages bears from feeding on the unhealthy garbage.

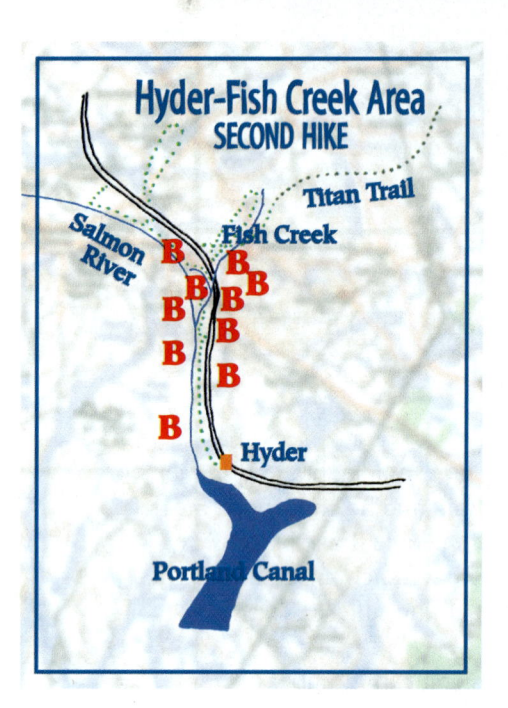

Bears don't understand the concept of borders, so some problems will inevitably arise until the bear sanctuary is extended to the Canadian side of the border. I have continued to press for discussions between the British Columbia Environment Department and the Alaskan Fish and Wildlife Department in the hope that a more extensive bear sanctuary can be created. This part of North America is blessed with a large bear population, which should be allowed to thrive amid the astoundingly beautiful scenery of the Fish Creek–Hyder region.

11

Denali National Park, Alaska

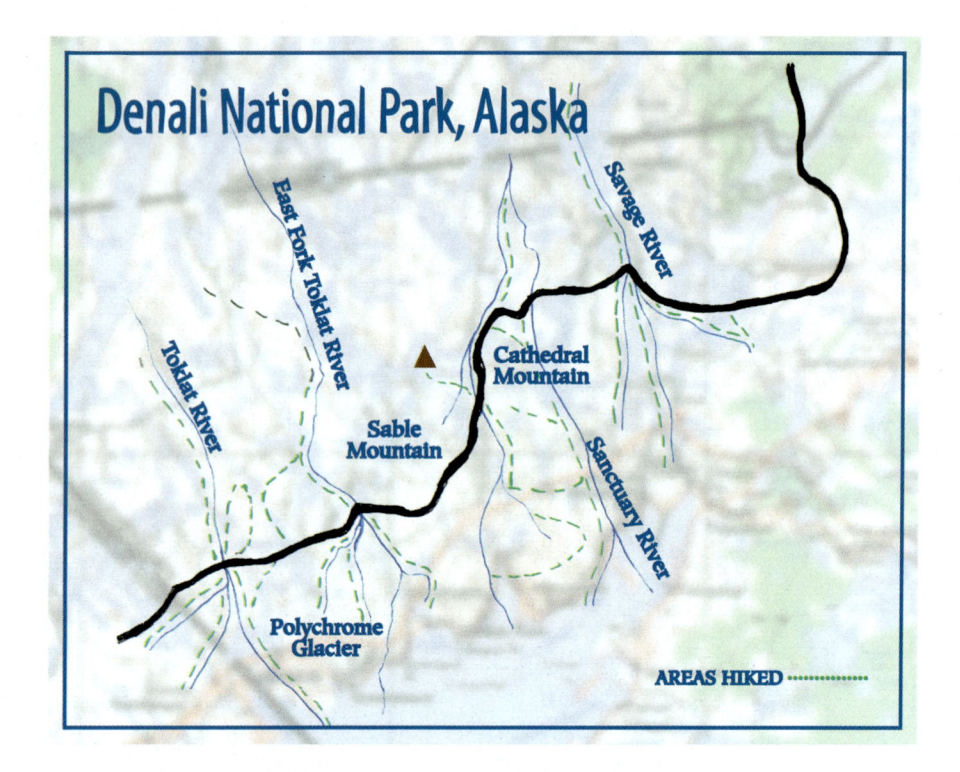

Denali is a very picturesque region of Alaska, and the national park, situated inland between the cities of Anchorage and Fairbanks, is well known for its large bear population. I have always felt drawn to revisit this area, and I finally did so in the summer of 1991.

Park officials are very safety-conscious in this area, and they always urge campers to use the triangle method. With this advice in mind, I began my first hike up Tatler Creek. School buses supplied by the federal government take tourists up and back the eighty-kilometre-long gravel road through the park every hour during the summer. The trip costs three dollars and takes eight hours. I got off the bus about one-third of the way along the road, directly north of Cathedral Mountain, and hiked three kilometres up Tatler Creek. The scenery is spectacular, especially when the trail rises above the tree line. Most of this park is alpine zone, so this is one of the best areas in the world to see grizzlies, caribou, and dall sheep. With few trees in the area, I could see the dall sheep on the high mountain tops, and with blueberries abundant on the hillsides, I knew I was camping where grizzlies would be roaming. I set up camp that evening on a ridge with a marvellous view—and remembered to place my gear well away from my tent and campfire, despite the visual distractions that surrounded me.

The next morning, I woke up to the pattering of a light rain. Dark clouds were blanketing the mountain tops, probably cousins of the Portal Creek rain cloud. The tallest mountain in North America, Mount McKinley (6,193 metres) stands between Anchorage and Fairbanks. It makes its own weather: a normal summer consists of rain or snow with the sun appearing every sixth day or so. But by noon on this day, the sun had beaten the clouds away. I hiked down to the stream and followed a trail parallel to a small creek. An adult grizzly emerged from behind a hill and immediately charged me. I stood still, hoping he was just testing me. When the bear was about twenty metres away, he veered off to my right; it had indeed been a bluff.

It is not unusual for a bear to come running towards an unwanted visitor, then abruptly stop and retreat. Bears do this to see if the intruder will run, which would be futile, because bears are extremely fast. If I had run, the bear would have become even more excited and would soon have had me for lunch. It is difficult to remain calm as you watch a charging bear, but this is the key to survival.

The grizzly was beside the stream, and behind him I noticed a caribou carcass. This explained why he had charged; my presence was perceived as an intrusion into his feeding spot, and he was trying to scare me off. I had interfered with him as he dined, and I, like any other animal that might have inadvertently wandered into his territory, had to be dealt with summarily.

I slowly backed away to a nearby ridge, where I could safely observe the bear and his meal. I noticed blood on the caribou; this meant the bear had probably killed the animal within the past few hours. A few moments later, a silver fox strolled along the shoreline of the creek; the bear saw it and charged. I sympathized with the fox. Nevertheless, the fox quickly retreated and the bear returned to his food.

Denali National Park.

Fifteen minutes later, the fox was back once again; apparently it had not understood the first message—or else it was too hungry to care. The grizzly, unaware that the interloper had returned, continued to eat. The fox manoeuvred around the grizzly and began to approach from the opposite side. This foolish fox was trying to sneak up on the carcass, but all he managed to do was get himself into a face-to-face encounter with the grizzly. This time, all the bear had to do was glare at the pesky would-be thief, which finally clued in and retreated, making its way upstream through the bushes. Tired of being disturbed, the grizzly lay down and went to sleep. The sun was dipping below the mountains, so I returned to my campsite.

The next day, the familiar-looking clouds were back. I kept an eye on the threatening sky as I began to hike along the bank of the Toklat River; I was now eighteen kilometres from Tatler Creek with spectacular alpine meadows in any direction I chose to hike. I was on a steep, grassy slope when I noticed a grizzly standing on his hind legs about thirty metres away. He looked at me for a moment, then dropped down and headed out of sight. Not as exciting as the day before, but better than nothing.

I continued hiking and was in front of a grassy knoll, when I heard a grunting noise. Two young grizzlies appeared and began walking towards me. I slowly began to move to my left, but even this controlled movement excited one of the bears, which broke into a run. When he was twelve metres away, I realized he was not bluffing; this bear was going to come all the way.

I immediately dropped to the ground and protected my head with my hands and arms. This was more excitement than I had counted on: the bear was right beside me, and I was an easy target.

A nervous Keith Scott.

But I guess I didn't smell very appetizing, because after the bear had sniffed most of my body, he ran to the hillside to join his companion. I was very nervous, but I sat up. The two bears were still within sight, but in a few moments they had both disappeared. It took me several days to stop shaking.

Later that week, while I was hiking near the Sable Mountains, I spotted a grizzly sow with two cubs. Fully recovered from my previous encounter, I watched the family with keen interest. They were feeding on some nearby grass and berries, but the sow appeared agitated and began pacing rapidly, her nose close to the ground. Then she got extremely excited, stood on her hind legs and looked intently at some rocks. The quick movements of the mother bear got the cubs excited too, and they began to circle their mother.

Finally I figured out what the mother bear was looking at. Among the rocks was a ground squirrel, frantically darting away from the bear, as she jumped around the area in an attempt to trap her quarry. But the speedy squirrel had already made its getaway. The dissatisfied bear continued to sniff the rocks, attempting to regain the scent, but it was no use. At last, all three bears calmed down and went back to the berry-and-grass picnic.

I was not the only one watching these bears. On a hillside not far away, an adult grizzly boar was nervously keeping an eye on the events below. The boar was shedding his fur, and he looked rather shaggy, but the coat would grow back before cold weather set in. Finally, the boar began to move away, glancing back periodically to make sure nothing was coming after him.

Grizzly sow spotting a squirrel.

A few days later, I was hiking early along the shore of the Toklat River when I came upon a grizzly sow with two cubs, all feeding on soopalie berries. The two cubs were extremely large—almost the size of their mother—and I knew they would soon be on their own. Even the way the three were eating was a clue: the cubs occasionally approached the berry patch where the sow was feeding, but she clearly disliked this idea and stared at them forbiddingly whenever they approached. Faced by that cold stare, the offending cubs backed up and went to look for another berry patch. When it was time to leave, the sow took the lead and the cubs followed, about nine metres behind her; this gap was yet another indication that the sow wanted more space.

Not long afterwards, a grizzly boar came over to sample the soopalie berries. But something was bothering this bear. He walked over to a flimsy tree, turned around, and scratched his rear end against the trunk. Then he turned his attention to his upper back, giving it a good, long massage against the rough bark. I could see from his big smile that this grizzly was really enjoying himself.

While this was going on, a large sow with two yearling cubs walked into an adjacent berry patch. This was trouble brewing—the presence of the other bear was clearly making the cubs nervous. Every few moments, they stood on their hind legs and looked around the area while the boar, his scratching done, went back to the berries, unaware that he was getting closer and closer to the bear family. When he was within twelve metres of the cubs, the mother bear became furious and charged.

The chase was on: both bears went galloping like racehorses towards a nearby hill. Not until the boar had run up the hillside did the sow stop her pursuit and return to her cubs; the male grizzly, safe for the moment, sat down and watched the other bears with extreme caution.

Magpie near the carcass.

With their mother back safely, the cubs became playful, batting each other with their front paws, then standing on their hind legs and hugging. The family walked to another berry patch and the antics continued as the cubs tried to splash each other in the river. The mother bear, uninterested in the game, sat in the water and tried to cool off after her fun.

The grizzly sow was aware of my presence; at one point she stood on her hind legs and stared in my direction, clearly unhappy that I was watching her. Then she began to walk in my direction. After seeing what had happened earlier, I knew this bear was protective; it was definitely time for me to leave. I slowly backed away, looking back after about five minutes. No bears were in sight.

    I had hiked several kilometres when I saw a caribou bull resting on the trail. He was enormous, with a large set of antlers, but suitable for an animal of his size. I had to wonder how he could see with those great prongs growing right in front of his eyes. I suppose he had to get used to seeing the same view. I continued on, happy to have had such an excellent day viewing animals.

    The next morning, I woke up early and was surprised that there were no clouds. But I suspected they were somewhere waiting for me. I was about to begin hiking when I noticed a grizzly feeding on blueberries, so I watched him eat. An hour later, he finally had his fill, and sat down for a rest. It is always comical to see one of these massive creatures in a sitting position. But what made this one particularly amusing was that he was scratching himself at the same time. Insects often burrow into a bear's fur, causing a powerful itch, which the bear relieves by using its claws as a digging tool to remove the bugs.

Caribou bull.

    As the grizzly was departing, he came face to face with a younger bear, which he immediately charged. The young bear turned and ran up the hillside, his pursuer right behind him. The chase lasted for about ten minutes; finally the boar had to give in to the swiftness of youth. He may have been big, but he was not very fast.

    Moments later, I heard a "WHOOF." I turned around and discovered I was not alone; next to me in the berry patch was a large grizzly, who—for the time being—was staring at me. The warning sound was an indication that this bear did not want me in the area. I complied with his wishes and slowly moved away. Just as I escaped, a familiar storm cloud moved overhead and dumped its load on me. I think nature was trying to tell me something, but I'm not sure what it was. Some twist on the cloud with the silver lining, no doubt.

The nights were becoming cooler now, and this made the wet, cloudy days even less tolerable than usual. However, the damp weather could not extinguish the beauty of the foliage. The once-green grass had mellowed to become a bright gold, and the willow leaves were turning orange, tinged with red. The landscape was like a rainbow, and the pot of gold was just being there to witness it.

It is during this time of year that members of the deer family rub the velvet skin off their antlers, and, for the bears, this is feasting season. With winter approaching, it is time to load up on food. The blueberry crop is starting to diminish, and the bears turn to soopalie berries, legumes, hedysarum roots, or bear roots as a staple of their daily diet. In addition, they begin to spend more time chasing ground squirrels to supplement the roots and berries.

Bull moose rubbing velvet off his antlers.

A few days passed before I saw another bear—a grizzly sow with two yearling cubs. They were walking across a meadow early one afternoon, stopping every once in awhile if they spotted some blueberries. The cubs seemed more interested in playing than eating. Whenever they were within striking distance of each other, a chase would commence and the young bears would wrestle each other and roll around on the ground. As a finale, they would bat each other with their paws. Then it would start all over again.

The sow, unconcerned with the cubs' shenanigans, sat down next to a berry patch and began eating. She periodically lifted her head and looked in the direction of the cubs, but after assuring herself that they were all right, she would turn back to her feast. Eventually, the mother bear stood up and began walking across a slope; then, with a sudden burst of speed, she broke into a run, stopped abruptly, and hit the ground with her front paws.

The object of all this attention was a series of squirrel holes, less than two metres away. Slowly, the sow approached the burrows, her nose close to the ground, then once again darted forward and skidded to a stop. Her best efforts proved inadequate that day; it seemed these bears would have to be content with a supper of berries.

Meanwhile, the cubs were trying to catch up to their mother. When they reached her side, all three started walking downhill, towards Sanctuary River. The water was quite high, but the eight-month-old cubs and the sow had no trouble crossing. On the other side was a large patch of soopalie berries, and soon the bears were enjoying a big meal.

After sampling the berries, the sow wandered over to a nearby tree and tried to relieve her itchy back. The cubs watched, then followed suit, rubbing against adjacent trees as their mother sat down and began to roll in the fine gravel beside the water. All of a sudden, the sow uttered two low-pitched grunting sounds, and the cubs quickly ran to her side.

The next thing I knew, all three bears began to walk towards me, wading across the stream. Now they were looking directly at me; the cubs appeared nervous, and one of them stood on its hind legs behind the sow. When she was about six metres away, I tried to slowly back up, hoping that I would not excite her. The sow walked over to where I had been standing, then began to feed on berries. Her actions were a way of conveying a message to me, and I received it loud and clear. If I had not responded as she wished, I am certain that she would have moved me herself.

One of the most interesting aspects of this bear family was the method of communication between the sow and her cubs. Each time the sow made two low grunts, the cubs immediately came to her side.

They never ignored this command—and, to tell the truth, I wouldn't have, either.

The sun was beginning to set, and, facing a four-kilometre hike back to the tent, I decided it was time to go. I took one last look at the three bears, then set out on my journey. Along the way, I had to cross Sanctuary River; the water had risen considerably, and I knew what to expect. Nothing to do but clench my teeth and wade in. It was terribly cold, the water was over my knees, and worst of all, I almost got swept away by the strong current. It took all my strength and balance to stay on my feet. Crossing streams and rivers has never been one of my favourite activities, and this experience reinforced my attitude.

Grizzly standing.

The next day, I spotted the same grizzly family in an alpine meadow. My presence made the bears nervous, and soon they were all running away. The grizzly sow was quick, and the young cubs were unable to keep up, although they ran as fast as they could. Eventually, the sow slowed down and took a look behind her. Because I was farther away, she came to a halt and waited for the cubs.

When they got to her side, she lay down and rolled over on her back. The cubs crawled on top of her and began to nurse. From my vantage point, the bears looked like a large boulder. The nursing lasted for about three minutes; then the sow got up on all fours and led her family away. I watched until all three bears disappeared over a hill.

Denali Mountain.

  The next morning, a light rain was falling in the valley, and as I hiked into the meadow, it started to snow. After about four hours, the sun finally broke through, the clouds dissipated, and I got my first clear view of Denali Mountain.
  Animals walking in winter landscapes are wonderful to watch. In a valley below, I noticed two caribou bulls pushing away snow with their hoofs, attempting to clear a small patch of grass to feed on. Their antlers were magnificent, and one caribou had ten points on each side of his.
  A few hours later, a chocolate-coloured grizzly walked in front of me, and, like the caribou, cleared a patch of grass with his front paw and began to eat. This bear did not object to my presence; in fact, he ignored me as he filled up on grass then ambled away.
  I stayed in the area for another night, but when I awoke, a snowstorm was in full swing. Nature's message was loud and clear, so I packed up my gear and returned to civilization. It had been an excellent trip, despite the weather.

12
Polar Bear Country

Near Churchill, Alaska

HUDSON BAY

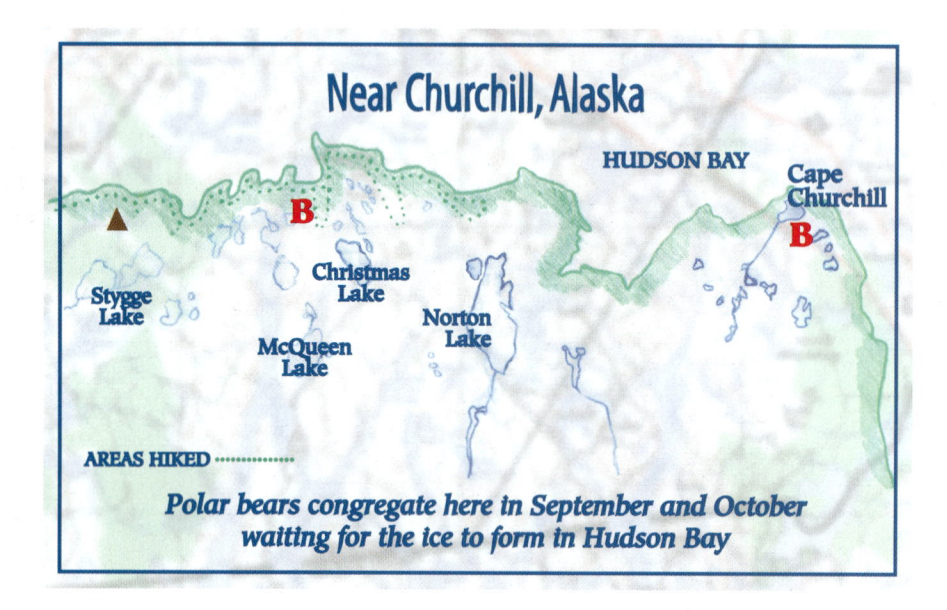

Cape Churchill

B

B

Stygge Lake

Christmas Lake

McQueen Lake

Norton Lake

AREAS HIKED ············

Polar bears congregate here in September and October waiting for the ice to form in Hudson Bay

Although I have been

photographing and studying bears for many years, I have always hesitated to travel north, to the Arctic. The pictures of polar bears I had seen were very nice, but I couldn't help noticing all the snow and ice they live in. From my point of view, there is only one thing worse than hiking in wet weather—hiking in cold weather.

I probably would never have set out at all, but one October I stopped thinking rationally and decided to go. I travelled to Thompson, Manitoba, then caught the train that would take me to the frigid north country.

When I got off the train in Churchill, Manitoba, the temperature was below my tolerance level, and there was a cold wind blowing in from Hudson Bay. Churchill, founded in 1700, is a small village with a population of less than one thousand. It is located in the northern part of the province at the mouth of the Churchill River, overlooking Hudson Bay. The village consists of a mall, a school, restaurants, a community centre and public library, a hospital, motels, an Eskimo museum, and an airport. There are no highways leading to Churchill; one must arrive by either plane, helicopter, or train. The main industry in Churchill is tourism.

Churchill is the polar bear capital of the world, and it isn't unusual for residents to see polar bears in their village. Because of this, I didn't see anyone walking too far from their homes while I was there. Although other wildlife is abundant in this area, polar bears remain the primary tourist attraction in this northern town.

In June and July, over two hundred species of birds are found on the tundra around Churchill, among them, the snowy owl, plovers, gyrfalcons, ducks, ivory gulls, Ross' gulls, ptarmigans, and geese. If you are lucky, you may see foxes, lemmings, or a wandering caribou.

There was already almost eight centimetres of snow on the ground when I arrived, and the people I passed looked at me oddly, probably because I was carrying a large pack on my back—an unusual sight at this time of year. I ignored the cold and the stares and hiked until I found an isolated spot to set up my tent. Then I had lunch. My sandwich was frozen.

I decided to hike along the shore of Hudson Bay. It was very cold, but there was no snow, only large, windswept boulders. The wind in this area is constant, which prevents any significant amounts of snow from accumulating, except in a few places beside the rocks. In one of these snowy spots, I noticed fox tracks and several ptarmigan feathers— probably the prey of that fox. I continued walking, and there was an Arctic fox, looking straight at me. He must have assumed I was not a threat, because he ignored me and continued on his way.

A few moments later I came to a very long beach; about halfway across, I noticed another fox, which had found a pocket of snow and was curled up asleep. I probably wouldn't even have noticed the fox because the fur was almost the same colour as the snow—winter camouflage for this and many other Arctic animals. But just as I passed by, the fox's dark eyes opened and it stared at me for a moment before dozing off again.

The sun did not appear very often on my first day, and the few times it did, I raced for my camera to take some pictures of the ominous landscape. It was difficult to get good photographs because in every direction the view was similar: a flat, windy, white landscape, like a vast

Hudson Bay in October.

desert of snow. I returned to my tent and unsuccessfully tried to get warm.

The next morning, I got up early. Snow was falling lightly, and there was a light wind. In this part of the world, such weather is considered excellent, and I have to admit that by that afternoon, I was really beginning to enjoy the area. I had hiked almost seven kilometres and was halfway down a beach when I noticed some recent polar bear tracks in the snow, leading towards the thick brush bordering the beach. I was not cold, but I began to shake—with anticipation.

I searched for a good lookout position and was soon seated on a hill that provided an excellent view of the surrounding area. I saw nothing move, so I returned to the tent. Two days out in the Arctic, and all I had seen was bear tracks. I knew I had to be patient, but I was beginning to wonder if I would ever get to see a polar bear. That night, as I crawled into my refrigerated sleeping quarters, it began to seem doubtful whether this trip was worth the effort.

The following day I got up and walked into town, my enthusiasm on ice. I tried to force myself to smile, but the wintry landscape was beginning to depress me. It was now time to try a new approach, so I decided to travel on one of the tour buses. The locals call these vehicles tundra buggies, and they look like large school buses with huge wheels that turn on tracks. The best feature of these buses is that they have powerful heaters.

I was cosy inside the bus, and the welcome warmth alone suggested that my luck was changing. The trip was bumpy, and for the first hour the only animals were some ptarmigans and two Arctic foxes—but then it happened. The bus pulled up beside a polar bear. Its fur was almost the exact colour as the surrounding snow, and it—she, actually—weighed about 135 kilograms. The young bear gazed calmly at our oddly shaped vehicle; apparently, polar bears in this area see these buses on a regular basis and realize that they don't pose a threat.

The area where the bus stopped would be this polar bear's home until the ice in Hudson Bay froze, after which she and her kind would begin to hunt seals on the ice. The mother of this bear probably brought her to the area long ago, and by instinct she will bring her back every year, just before the ice freezes.

Playful polar bears.

Just beyond the spot where we had seen the first bear, I noticed two others. These polar bears were much larger, about 225 kilograms, and they were standing on their hind legs, hugging each other. Every few seconds, they tried to swat each other with their paws—just as I had seen the grizzly cubs do. The wrestling match continued for about twenty minutes, with no clear victor.

Soon, a third bear approached to settle the dispute. After the three had played around for a few minutes, they began grinning at each other as if they were trying to show off their teeth.

An hour passed, and now I could see the bears everywhere I looked, some of them pale yellow, but most of them white. The biggest one we came across weighed about 360 kilograms, and he gave everyone in the bus a scare when he trotted over, stood on his hind legs, and stared in the window. Many of the passengers fell silent as the bear looked them over and drooled on the window frame.

Wrestling polar bears.

Soon afterward, another one came over to the bus, lay down, and rolled up into a ball—that's the way polar bears go to sleep. And then, right beside the sleeping bear, another large bear came over and began scratching his neck and his head, first from side to side, then in a vertical motion. Finally, he stretched his neck and stuck his nose straight up in the air. So far, these bears were putting on an excellent show.

As I watched them, I began to consider the difficulties I would encounter if I tried to hike in this area. The bears were almost the exact colour of the snow and a hiker could easily stumble over one, mistaking it for a drift.

But I didn't dwell on these thoughts for very long. There was too much to see. Two polar bears were pushing each other in the snow, and they began wrestling. A third joined in, and after a short battle, the polar bears sat down and then pawed and bit each other's faces.

After a few more minutes of wrestling, one of the playful bears blew

Polar bear sleeping.

air through his nose in a loud snort that could be heard by everyone on the bus. This sound must have been a signal that something was about to happen, because the others began to move away from the bear that had snorted. The lone bear moved its bowels, and one of its neighbours came over and ate the droppings. A few moments later, the playful mood returned, and the bears went back to wrestling. I noticed that when they were running, they bounded gracefully, rather like cats.

The passengers attempted to count all the polar bears near our vehicle—seventeen. It was remarkable to see so many of these magnificent animals in such a small area, and it was a sight I will never forget.

The next morning, I crawled out of my tent at daybreak and began to hike along the coastline. By noon, I came to an area where there were recent polar bear tracks. Unfortunately, the snow was starting to fall, and this limited my visibility to less than fifteen metres. I kept repeating to myself, "The weather will not defeat me." I was extremely nervous during this storm; polar bears were difficult to spot during good weather, and they would be impossible to spot in such a storm. I was already beginning to feel defeated.

Thankfully, the storm soon subsided, and I was able to see a bit farther ahead. The snow had stopped just in time; there in front of me was a polar bear, sitting on the trail. I remained motionless, hoping the bear would not see me, and then I realized that its eyes were closed. This bear was sleeping in a sitting position.

I continued to watch, and a few moments later, the bear yawned, rolled onto its side and went back to sleep. A few more minutes passed before it awoke fully, sat up, yawned, then looked sideways and stuck out its tongue.

This polar bear was acting oddly, and I did not think it would be wise to push my luck. I had already experienced the most exciting encounter of my journey, a glimpse of a polar bear without my safety ensured by the protection of a bus. The bear had not yet sensed my presence, and I wanted to keep it that way, so I slowly backed away. On the way back to my tent, I paused frequently to see if I were being pursued; luckily, I was not.

That night I almost froze to death, and the next day I took the first train back to civilization. The weather had been as tough as I always imagined, but the trip was definitely worth the pain.

13

The Bear Man's Safety Rules

Roadside Bears

The most likely bear encounter anyone will experience is from behind the windows of a car. It is not uncommon for black bears or grizzlies to travel along roads or in ditch areas, mainly because they are frequently fed by motorists. Feeding the bears encourages them to return for more food. However, bears that are fed will soon lose their fear of humans, and this is how unfortunate incidents occur. It does not take much effort for a bear to bite the hand that feeds it—so don't feed the bears.

Furthermore, this practice endangers the lives of hikers, who might come across a bear that has come to associate humans with a source of food. If no handout is forthcoming, the hiker might have to deal with an angry bear—not a desirable state of affairs.

Taking Pictures

Anyone who enjoys taking pictures of bears must exercise caution. I once saw a tourist with a small box camera get out of his car and run to within ten metres of a bear, in a foolish attempt to get a close-up shot. Instead of posing, the bear responded by charging the man. I hollered, and this momentarily distracted the bear, allowing the tourist to escape.

The problem with this tourist's approach was that he had to get close to the bear to obtain his photograph. A much safer way to get a close-up is to use a telephoto lens; in fact, this is an essential piece of equipment for anyone interested in photographing bears—and living long enough to get the pictures developed.

Photographers should also keep in mind that stooping over to take a picture might lead a bear to think you are about to charge him. This is a

Taking pictures with a telephoto lens.

threat that bears will respond to, and a bear responding to a threat is not a pretty sight. It cannot be emphasized enough that one must not appear threatening to a bear, and that one must always take pictures from a safe distance. If a bear approaches, back away. Do not worry about objects that are left behind.

Getting Ready For Bear Country

Plans for a trip to a provincial, state, or national park should begin with a call to park officials and a query about the most recent bear sighting in the area you intend to visit. If there is a large amount of bear activity reported, a change in plans is in order; best to avoid this area. Even if no bears have been reported in an area, do not conclude that there are none around.

Usually, a bear that sees or smells a human will avoid contact and leave the area. Problems normally arise from surprise meetings; for example, a hiker may come around a bend and suddenly come face to face with a bear. Trouble can arise from these collisions. Also keep in mind that bears often blend in very well with their surroundings. I have often stared at what I believed was a large rock—and then the rock would get up and begin to move. When hiking, cautiously approach turns in the trail and pay close attention to the details of the landscape.

Preparations for a hiking trip should include several precautions that, if followed, will reduce the likelihood of a bear encounter. I have studied Parks Canada safety precautions and tested them in Banff National Park from 1980 to 1985. Here is the best advice I have tested.

One of the most important steps is *not* to carry any strong-smelling foods into the woods. Avoid meat products, especially bacon or fish; instead, bring freeze-dried or powdered foods. Also worth leaving behind are perfumes, scented soaps, lipsticks, make-up, and shaving cream. Anyone with a wound should pay particular attention, and wash it well to remove the smell of blood.

I once sprinkled perfume on some rocks, then climbed a nearby tree and waited to see what would happen. Within two hours, a grizzly sow and her cubs approached the area. I returned to the rocks the following day to discover the rock had been completely overturned. Bears have an excellent sense of smell, and strong odours make them curious. The last thing a hiker wants is a curious bear coming toward him.

Bear spray.

The risk to hikers is greatly reduced if they take a can of bear spray into the woods. Recently, several bear sprays such as Counter Assault have become popular, and these do repel bears. When the spray is discharged, it is effective against a bear up to 5.8 metres away. The spray severely irritates the animal's eyes, nose, and skin, and it is not uncommon for a sprayed bear to immediately collapse. The effects of the spray last about an hour, after which the bear will wander away. The spray does no permanent damage to the bear—if it did, I would not carry it. Carrying bear spray when you hike will also provide nervous hikers with psychological comfort; in the event that they do encounter a bear, the impulse to run will be lessened.

Bear bells are another useful piece of equipment, especially in areas with a large bear population. Tied to a backpack during a hike, they will jingle constantly, alerting bears that there is a human nearby and discouraging them from approaching. If bear bells are not available, a tin can with rocks tied to it will have the same effect. But remember that near a stream, the sounds of rushing water may drown out even the loud ringing of the bells; it is a good idea to sing or talk loudly in this situation so that bears will hear the unwelcome noise and depart. Some hikers carry a small boat horn, which they blow if they see signs of a bear, but under normal circumstances, bear bells are adequate.

Hiking in Bear Country

While on the trail, look for signs that may indicate the presence of a bear. The sight or smell of a dead animal should be a signal to circle the area or back away. The sound of croaking ravens, chattering squirrels, or running animals may also signify the presence of a nearby bear, so listen intently while travelling through the woods.

A trail with a hump in the centre indicates a path that is frequently used by bears. The pads of bears' paws wear down the trail, leaving a raised area running down the centre. Another indicator is a large number of depleted berry bushes along a trail; bears often feed on berries along the path. Never interrupt a bear that is eating—back away, slowly and calmly.

Indeed, the very presence of a berry patch should prompt caution; after bears eat, they frequently rest nearby. During the berry season, bear droppings—which resemble those of cows—contain undigested berries, which can be red, orange, blue, or black. Another problem with being in a berry patch is that a bear may think an interloper is trying to steal its food, and this will cause it to become aggressive. Finally, while hiking in an area that has a salmon stream, be on the lookout for overturned rocks, bear tracks, or recently killed salmon—all signs of bear activity.

If children are participating in the hike, be certain that everyone stays close together; a good idea is to encourage them to walk between adults.

Bear droppings.

Even if there are no children, try not to get too far from one another. A rule of thumb is to stay within sight of another member of your party at all times. If hiking alone, inform local officials of your activity so they will know where to find you if anything goes wrong. If possible, stick to trails that are open enough to allow you to see at least nine metres ahead. Bears, like humans, prefer trails to struggling through the bush.

It is also important to know bears' resting patterns. They are most active just before dark and early in the morning, so try to avoid hiking at these times. The fall of the year is also a very active time for bears and more care is necessary when hiking during this season. Siesta time is usually between eleven in the morning and three in the afternoon. During this period be alert for sleeping bears, and keep a careful eye on the ground while walking in a densely forested area. Bears also tend to be inactive on warm days, when they go looking for shady areas where they can rest. And, of course, the winter months mean hibernation, but some bears sleep more soundly than others, so don't be surprised if you see one in January.

Female Hikers

For women, the menstrual period is not a good time to be hiking in an area where bears live. They have an extremely acute sense of smell and can easily detect blood. If a woman does choose to hike at this time, she should take extra precautions. I once put blood on a piece of cotton and placed it near a bear trail. The cotton was gone the next day and bear scratches and tracks were evident.

Whistling in Bear Country

It is not a good idea to whistle while hiking. Bears may think they're hearing marmots, one of their favourite foods. The call of a marmot is very similar to a human whistle, and the noise will at the very least make a bear curious. I was not always certain that whistling was a bad idea, but after several encounters, like the one in the Jasper area, I can verify that whistling does not scare a bear away. It has the opposite effect. I have whistled when grizzlies were nearby, and they still approached me. Since an approaching bear is bad news, don't whistle.

Hiking and the Wind

Wind direction is an important factor to consider when travelling in bear country. It is more dangerous to hike downwind of a bear, because the scent will be easier to detect. If the wind is at your back, then heighten your awareness of what is in front of you. A wind blowing in your face will not carry your scent quite as readily—but check behind you from time to time, just to be sure.

Camping in Bear Country

Always be careful when selecting a campsite. Provincial or state parks usually have designated camping areas and require that these be used; one cannot simply pitch a tent anywhere along the trail. Although these sites are chosen with safety in mind, some of them are unsafe. Be especially wary of a campground where food-storage and eating areas are located less than ninety metres from the tenting area. Bears can smell food, even the lingering odours of food, and they will investigate the attractive smells.

Another sign of trouble is an area overrun with squirrels and chipmunks. The presence of many small animals indicates that humans have been feeding them, and they have lingered in hopes of getting more food. The animals themselves—or even the scattered crumbs—may be enough to attract a bear, so avoid campsites with a lot of activity.

If there is an outhouse at the campground, make sure it does not have a strong odour. Unlike human urine, which is repulsive to bears, the smell of human excrement will attract them, and I have even seen them eating it. If there is no outhouse, then walk a considerable distance from the tent to defecate; otherwise the smell may attract a nearby bear.

The condition of the camping area is another important consideration. If there is garbage strewn about, the campground should be avoided. Abandoned garbage strongly attracts bears.

When I go camping, I always check for bear tracks, claw marks on trees, or deep holes left by bears digging for squirrels.

If I see these kinds of signs, I usually sleep in a hammock high above the ground. To keep from falling out of the airborne bed, tie a rope around yourself and attach it to a tree limb. I have spent almost two summers sleeping in a hammock and can report that I was comfortable and safe.

A hole resulting from a grizzly pursuing a squirrel.

Cooking and Storing Food

When you are camping, it is essential to store and cook food properly. The triangle method is the best way to ensure safe camping—sleeping, eating, and food-storage areas should be kept at least ninety metres apart. This is an excellent way to prevent food odours from drifting towards you as you doze. The last thing a camper wants is a hungry bear in the tent, trying to get at some food. A few cooking precautions are also helpful: remember that bears are most active at daybreak and twilight, so plan meals accordingly; and keep in mind that the delicious smell of frying fish or meat is just as appealing to a bear as to a hiker, so use caution.

Ideally, a bear-resistant container should be used to store food, and the safety-conscious officials at parks such as Denali in Alaska provide these to hikers free of charge. Otherwise, seal the food tightly in a plastic bag, making certain there are no openings through which odours might escape.

The safest place to keep food is up in the air—literally. Tie a rope between two trees, at least six metres above the ground, then attach another rope to the food bag or container and extend it to the middle of the line. If the food container is properly sealed, a bear that walks under the bag will not detect any odours. If you are camping in an area that has no trees, then seal the food and stash it among some rocks.

It is not uncommon to hear noises outside a tent late at night. If it seems likely that a bear is nearby, make some noise—talk loudly or sing. This noise will usually scare off any nearby animals. Do not get out of the tent to investigate if you believe that a bear has taken your food during the night because this will greatly increase your risk. If a bear has obtained food he will usually rest nearby and protect it, so wait until the morning to check.

Despite the best precautions, it is possible that a bear will get your food anyway. He might climb the tree and knock down your food container, or overturn the rocks that were used as an alpine-zone hiding spot. Under no circumstances try to get your food back; the bear will win any property dispute. And try not to let the theft ruin your trip; just be happy that the food was not stored inside your tent.

I have had my food stolen by bears several times, but I never let it upset me. In one instance, a bear climbed a tree, ripped apart my line, stole my food and ran off. I could hear it all from my tent, but I did not interrupt the bear. Instead, I made the most of my trip by eating fish, berries, and roots for the next six days.

I have also been careless, and I always pay for it. On one occasion, I was camping at a government campground. In such places it is easy to assume that no bears will be around—but this is a false assumption, as I soon learned. I had placed my backpack on a picnic table just outside my tent and soon forgot about it. At about midnight, I heard some loud huffing sounds. I sat up and looked outside the tent. Much to my dismay, there was a large bear eating food from my torn pack.

The bear was close enough that I could have reached out and touched him, and for a moment I saw him stare directly at me: just another forgetful camper leaving freebies around. Because the bear was so close, I got nervous and decided my best option was to cut a hole in the back of the tent and make a cautious retreat. The bear was too interested in my cornflakes to bother with me; luckily, I made it to safety. But the incident taught me an important lesson. Never leave food near your tent, no matter how safe you believe it is.

Garbage Disposal in Bear Country

If your food successfully makes it through the night, the next issue to consider is garbage. Food waste attracts bears, so it is important to put all garbage in a plastic bag and seal it. Any combustible food cans that have been emptied should be burned to eliminate odours. If you are in an area where fires are prohibited, then use a plastic bag, sealing the cans tightly inside.

It is not a good idea to bury garbage in the woods, because bears will be able to detect the odours and dig the garbage up. More to the point, they will linger in the area, hoping for seconds. Another good reason not to bury the trash is that a can may harm a bear that digs it up and tries to lick the inside. Lastly, I believe the old saying: if a hiker is strong enough to carry food into the woods, he is strong enough to carry the garbage back out. The last thing anyone who loves nature wants to encounter is an area destroyed by human garbage.

Dogs in Bear country

There is one simple rule to remember about dogs in bear country: don't take them there. When unleashed dogs are in the woods, they invariably chase bears, which respond by chasing the terrified dogs right back to their masters. The ensuing encounter between maddened bear and puny human might have tragic results.

In August 1993, for example, two mushroom pickers were deep in the woods of northern British Columbia with a dog. The dog found a black bear and began to chase him, eventually returning to his master with the black bear in close pursuit. One of the men shot and wounded the bear, which, infuriated with pain, wrestled one of them to the ground and killed him.

Dog with bear bells.

The entire incident could have been avoided if the dog had been left behind; in fact, many provincial parks do not allow dogs on back-country trails for this very reason. If you must bring a dog, make sure it is on a leash.

Bear Dens

Hikers who come across a cave, or what looks like a bear den, should leave the area immediately. Hibernating bears have been seen roaming near their dens in winter; they can be awakened by nearby noise, and they may wander in the area, searching for food. Anything that moves in the snow is a potential meal for a bear; if you see a bear in the winter, slowly back away.

Fishing in Bear Country

Bears always have the right of way—especially around a fishing hole. If you see a bear approaching while you're fishing, cautiously back away from the area. If a bear should try for a fish being reeled in, cut the line.

Even without bears around, exercise great care in fishing. Make sure to clean your catch more than ninety metres from the tent. After the fish is cleaned, store it in a tightly sealed plastic bag and wash your hands thoroughly. Fish are one of a bear's favourite foods, and if your hands or clothes smell like a fish, a bear may pay you a visit—and he won't be happy with substitutions.

Encountering a Bear

On some trips, you may take all the precautions in the world, yet still see a bear. There are may ways to reduce risks. The danger is at its worst if you are within fifty metres of the bear, which may react by making popping sounds with its teeth, or by turning sideways and appearing to ignore you. These are indications that the bear wants you to leave, and you would be wise to comply.

Within a fifty-metre range, a bear can see and smell you, and it is important to back away slowly in these cases. If you are on a trail and a bear approaches, cautiously and calmly get off the trail and give the bear plenty of space to pass. Near a lake or a river, wade into the water as far as you can; this will discourage the bear from giving chase. If you encounter a resting bear, back up and leave the area.

Never, never, never run away from a bear. Running will only excite the bear, and it will chase whatever is moving. Bears are exceptionally fast runners. Once I stepped out of my car near Lake Louise to take a picture of a sow grizzly with her cubs, and she charged. I retreated into the car and drove away with the sow hot in pursuit. At one point she was actually gaining on me. Instead of running, stand your ground and use slow movements as you back away; your best defence is to remain calm.

The temptation to run can sometimes overpower clear thinking, and I have seen this happen many times. On one occasion, I was out on the trail with two very experienced hikers, Jim Kahl and Doug Hall. Two large grizzlies suddenly appeared, walking towards us. Jim and Doug turned to run; I grabbed them and told them to remain still. The bears looked at us for a while, then turned and wandered away. Jim and Doug had behaved instinctively, but in this situation it is better to go against any feelings of panic and remain calm. Slow movements help to keep the bear calm, and this will greatly reduce the risk of an attack.

If you encounter a bear cub, realize the danger. A mother bear is very protective of her cubs, and she will react instantly if she hears one of them whine. The sow may not be immediately visible, but rest assured—she is nearby. Again, slowly back away and leave the area.

The worst possible bear encounter for a hiker to experience is to be caught between a sow and her cubs. It is highly likely that the sow will determine your fate. The sight of a charging bear will probably numb your thought processes, but try to remember that running is futile. Stand your ground; the bear may stop, look you over and then retreat. This will mean that she has only bluffed a charge, and you will

Sleeping bear.

Two aggressive black bears.

Grizzly.

have been extremely lucky.

If the bear keeps coming, do not panic. Use bear spray, if you have it, when the bear is within spraying distance. If you don't have it, drop to the ground and roll up like a ball, protecting your head. Stay completely still. I have had to do this on three occasions, and the charging bear has always reacted by sniffing my body and then leaving. A sow's first priority is to protect her cubs, and she will want to return to them as quickly as possible. The combination of a non-threatening position and a bear's tendency to be repulsed by the smell of human beings, encourages the sow to make a hasty departure.

If a bear does begin to maul you, now is the time to panic. Fight vigorously if your assailant is a black bear; it may react to your behaviour by retreating. However, if the bear is a grizzly, your chances of fighting him off are minimal.

Hunting Bears

I do not support bear hunting, but I realize that it does occur and will unfortunately continue. An injured bear always reacts by becoming aggressive in an attempt to protect itself. I do not blame bears for responding in this way; I believe injuries to hunters are often a result of their own inexperience: if they provoke an attack, they must be prepared to accept the unfortunate consequences.

Hiking Near Polar Bears

If you should ever happen to find yourself hiking in the Arctic (you never know), there are several warning signs to remember about polar bears. An angry polar bear will blow air out of its nose; if you are nearby, the unusual sound is impossible to miss. Bears trying to acquire a scent will move their head and neck from side to side; if you see these movements, back up and leave the area.

If you encounter a polar bear and are close enough to make a cautious retreat to a car or cabin, then do so—keeping in mind the fact that a bear will notice a moving object more readily than a stationary one. If the polar bear follows, drop your pack, jacket, or any other items that might attract its attention. A polar bear will often stop to check unusual objects; while the bear satisfies its curiosity, you can make your getaway.

The best way to watch polar bears is from a safe place, such as the tundra tour buses, which have the additional benefit of drivers who are very friendly and informative.

Report Bear Sightings

When hiking in parks, report bear sightings to park officials so other hikers can take precautions. If one official seems to ignore your volunteer information, try speaking with another. Safety from bears is an important concern for everyone visiting a park.

Living in Bear Country

An obvious precaution for a bear country resident to take is to be careful with garbage. Never leave it out overnight or store it near a residence. If a bear finds garbage once, it will return on a regular basis, and this can lead to trouble. Some municipalities now have bear-proof garbage containers, and these eliminate most of the problems.

For many years, bears freely raided the unprotected garbage at dumps. Many bears would become dependent on this food and turn away from their natural diet; this led to a great many health problems among the bears. Another concern was the encounters between humans and bears in dump areas; many communities have since enclosed their dumps with electric fences, making them virtually bear-proof. The bear receives only a slight shock that deters it from returning to the dump area. In my opinion, this is a positive move and one of the ways municipalities can help bears.

Transporting a grizzly to a remote area.

If a town is being visited by a large number of bears, residents should contact wildlife officials so that the bears can be tranquillized and safely transported to a remote area.

In almost every case of a confrontation between a bear and a human being, there is a tendency to condemn the bear. However, this is not always justified; people do not always take the proper precautions around bears. If they do, I believe they greatly reduce the risk of bear confrontation and subsequent human injury will be greatly reduced.

There will never be a guarantee of safety. Bears may be injured or have health problems such as bad teeth, and in such conditions bears are aggressive, moody, and unpredictable. Nevertheless, taking the proper precautions will give you confidence and keep you safer—making your visit to "bear country" much more enjoyable.